"If you want to know what it really mea[...] a must read. Greg offers practical frameworks for the key pillars of product management that you can put to work immediately. This book is destined to become the definitive guide on strategy for PMs."
Anant Chintamaneni, VP Products, BlueData, Inc.

"Good Product Managers know how to lead teams to ship product. But the great ones do more than that—they execute a true product strategy. This book is a much-needed primer on how to do exactly that."
Mike Belsito, Co-Founder of Product Collective and Co-Organizer of INDUSTRY: The Product Conference

"Read Greg's book before your competitors do: it's chock full of great frameworks and advice for how to take your strategic thinking to the next level."
Dan Olsen, Product Management Consultant and Author of *The Lean Product Playbook*

"When one of my favorite voices in agile told me there was a deficit on strategic thinking and an opportunity to fix it, I listened. I'm glad I read this book."
Alex Cowan, faculty, University of Virginia Darden School of Business

"With **Strategy Excellence for Product Managers**, Greg Cohen has created an outstanding guide for product and market-focused growth hackers who want to develop new professional skills or simply enhance existing ones. Exhaustively researched and peppered with fascinating real-world examples that bring strategy concepts to life, this compact volume packs a career's-worth of hard-won experience into an exceptional reference manual that readers will want to re-visit again and again."
John Armstrong, Growth hacker and Chief Marketing Officer, Zettaset

"Today a great deal of emphasis is placed on being responsive to the market. Greg Cohen's latest book illustrates how product managers can perform even better by being both responsive and strategic."
Sanjay Raghu, Head of Product Marketing & Technical Services, CloudGenera

Strategy Excellence

for Product Managers

A Guide to Winning
Markets through
Product Strategy

GREG COHEN

Strategy Excellence for Product Managers
A Guide to Winning Markets through Product Strategy

For permission requests, or for quantity purchases, write to the publisher at:

Agile Excellence Press
www.agile-excellence.com
sales@agile-excellence.com

WARNING AND DISCLAIMER
Although every effort has been taken to verify the accuracy of the information contained herein, the author and publisher assume no responsibility for any errors or omissions. The information in this book is distributed on an "as is" basis, without warranty. neither the author nor the publisher shall have any liability to any person or entity with respect to any loss or damage caused or alleged to be caused directly or indirectly by the information contained in this book.

TRADEMARKS
Trademarked names may appear throughout this book. Rather than use a trademark symbol with every occurrence of a trademarked name, names are used in an editorial fashion, with no intention of infringement of the respective owner's trademark.

Editing by Bill Hilton
Cover Design and Illustrations by Yasemin Akyuz
Interior Design by Stephanie Anderson

Published by: Agile Excellence Press an imprint of Agile Excellence LLC
Place of Publication: Silicon Valley, California, USA

First Printing: September 2017
Paperback ISBN 978-0-9991106-0-7
eBook ISBN: 978-0-9991106-1-4
Paperback Library of Congress Catalog Number: 2017913376

To all those dedicated to bringing great products to market.

ACKNOWLEDGEMENTS

This book is the culmination of my two decades in product management, both as a practitioner and a consultant. The recurring theme in my career has been the need to break down complex problems into recognizable patterns that can frame and guide decision making. I've worked with too many colleagues, mentors, clients and users to list all their names here. For anyone who has ever asked or answered a question related to product management, please know that you have influenced my thinking. The list below is a narrower one, of individuals who have contributed directly to this book or acted as a sounding board for my ideas over the years.

Thank you to my colleagues, past and present, at the 280 Group. It has been a privilege working with you. Also to Professor Jean-Pierre Jeannet, who first taught me how to analyze industries and gave me knowledge that I have used throughout my career; to John Konsin who trusted me with my first opportunities to solve difficult product problems through strategic analysis; to Alex Cowan and Dan Olsen, who have been partners in applying Lean theory to product management; to Rich Mironov for his never-ending insights; and to Luke Hohmann for introducing me to the power of visual facilitation, which led to a number of the techniques described in this book. Special thanks to Mike Lisavich for sharing his experiences with design sprints at Rekindle.

Thank you to Pam Schure, Phil Burton, and Roger Snyder for technical review. Special thanks to Brian Lawley, founder of the 280 Group, for the constant encouragement. Thank you to my editor Bill Hilton for making this book more readable, and to my graphic designer Yasemin Akyuz for cover design and illustrations.

Thank you Stephanie Anderson and the staff at Jera Publishing for layout and enduring many revisions. Thank you to the amazing team from CreateSpace for all your effort to get this book through the publishing process.

Lastly, thank you to my wife and children who support me and allow me the time to write.

CONTENTS

FOREWORD

Product managers from around the world, we have a problem. You and your teams are focused on delivering great new features as rapidly as possible and getting them into your customers' hands quickly, to give your product and company a short-term competitive advantage. We have more customer feedback, and are able to listen to the voice of the customer and respond to it better than at any time in history. And we have lean and agile processes and tools designed to support rapid time to market. So we get to work and crank out new features that customers want and need right now.

Sounds great, doesn't it? So what's the problem?

Think of it this way. You've promised to take your customers on a road trip in your car to a destination. You can get them there rapidly, and along the way you can provide them with all kinds of great benefits. Free Wi-Fi, a comfortable and safe vehicle to travel in and beautiful scenery along the way. Partway through the ride your competitor starts offering similar trips that include fresh-made espresso in the vehicle, so you add an espresso machine to your vehicle to compete. Another adds a drone that can capture a video of customers making the journey from outside of the car so that they can share the footage on social media, so you add this too. It seems like you are adding all of the features and benefits your customers could possibly want, and are adding them rapidly and innovating as you do it. And, short-term, your customers tell you that you are doing exactly what they want.

But what if the car they are in is going to the wrong destination? What if the destination changes as the trip progresses, and the trip you give your customers can't get them to where they need to go? What if the last fifty miles require a four-wheel drive vehicle, and you can't offer that in time? Or what if, while you are busy adding all of these incremental features, a competitor that you didn't even realize was in the same business as you builds a hyperloop? And what if customers can now get to the right destination fifty times faster and ten times cheaper, so that all of those cool new features and services you built no longer matter?

280 Group calls this coding or developing yourself into a corner (analogous to painting a room and realizing that you have painted yourself into a corner without watching what you were doing, so that now you can't get out without walking over wet paint). A "rush to features" can often be a rush to failure. And the bottom line is that you can code or develop the best features in the world, but if you don't have a good vision and strategy based on the bigger picture, it may not matter.

The ultimate gauge of great product management is whether the vision, strategy and long-term viability of the product is solid. This must take all factors into account — the market, trends, your company's core strengths and weaknesses, customer needs, customer wants, competitive factors, timing, the short-term financial goals your company must achieve and many more.

Who in your company can be cognizant of all of these to set the strategy and make sure that long-term the company and its products will succeed? Executive management can't — they are focused on running the company and don't have the lower-level details and data to set product strategy. Sales can't — they are focused on making the short-term tactical numbers. Engineering can't — they are focused on building products efficiently and using new technologies, but rarely have the business and customer knowledge to drive things from a bigger picture. Operations is focused on cutting costs and effectively delivering products, and Marketing is focused on getting the word out about what you have now.

The only function in a company that can drive strategy is Product Management. And let's face it, a mediocre product with a great strategy can win in the market long-term (just look at Microsoft, who dominated many markets for over 25 years with products that were "just good enough" yet had a strategy that set them up so no one could compete.) Or look at Nokia and RIM Blackberry, who had great products but flawed strategies, and went from massive success to failure rapidly.

In this book, Greg Cohen (who incidentally is one of the smartest product management people I know) gives you the insight, knowledge and tools to become a great strategic product thinker. I sincerely believe and hope that his thinking will change the course of not only your products, but your entire career.

Brian Lawley
CEO & Founder, 280 Group

INTRODUCTION

In 2000, I was working in Silicon Valley at the epicenter of the dot com mania. The cost of capital was rapidly approaching zero for startups and moving fast was all that mattered. My team was hard at work developing a product that would launch into a market that we were going to create. There was little precedent to guide us, and we needed flexibility and speed. To make this possible, the product team adopted a relatively unproven development methodology known as eXtreme programming. From that point on my life as a product manager was forever changed. The team could now incorporate real-time learning into the product plans. The company could nimbly zig and deftly zag and the product team was right there to support it. It was amazing.

Being part of a well-functioning Agile team was a formative experience. It turned me into a huge fan of Agile methods. I spoke at conferences and told anyone who would listen why Agile was the future. I wrote articles, blog posts, and even a bestselling book on Agile. I remain a champion of Agile practices.

It's been 17 years since that first introduction to eXtreme Programming. Agile methods, including the popular Scrum framework, are widely adopted across product teams in every industry. As I watch companies and engage with product teams, a new concern has emerged. Today I fear that product teams risk falling victim to the law of unintended consequences, when a purposeful change for the better leads to an unforeseen negative outcome.

Product teams experience such a high level of flexibility through Agile development that it is easy, even natural, to get caught up in the moment, to react to the immediate market signals you receive, and, in the excitement, to respond quickly.

This is deeply gratifying. But in the process the team, and the product manager, can overlook the hard work of strategy.[1]

To fill the gap, product owners were expected to articulate a vision.[2] The vision sat above the product backlog. The vision construct was intended to show the team where they were going, create alignment, and focus the team on the outcome of their work, not just on the output or velocity of their efforts. The vision would guide the team and keep them focused over the long-term.

Although vision creates a shared picture of the future, it does not take into account the fact that markets are dynamic. Markets are also filled with competitors that are actively trying to get between you and the customer, and impede the realization of your vision. More often than not, some of your competitors are bigger and better resourced than you.

Product strategy helps you navigate an uncertain and shifting market. It informs the vision as much as it is informed by the vision. Not all visions are achievable. Product strategy helps you figure out whether your vision is attainable or not.

Management guru Peter Drucker states in his book *Management* that "Strategic planning is not a box of tricks or a bundle of techniques. It is analytic thinking and commitment of resources to action". Thus, product strategy is the cerebral glue that holds the product plan together. It is where the majority of analytic thinking occurs. Then, for the portion of the product strategy that is realized through development, the product backlog represents the commitment of engineering resources to action.

Yahoo! — A Cautionary Tale

This is the story of rise and fall of Yahoo! and the belated attempts by a brilliant product leader to turn the company around. It touches upon both corporate and product strategy, highlighting the time frames and the interplay between the

---

1 Before Agile development, product managers had to master strategy. In the world of "waterfall" development, the product plan typically represented a commitment of one to three years. The plan had to be deeply considered and defensible.
2 It should be noted that articulating a product vision, while recognized as valuable, is not a defined responsibility of the product owner in the Scrum Guide.

two. Further, it demonstrates the limitations of Agile product planning when not supported by strong corporate and product strategy.

Yahoo! was founded by Jerry Yang and David Filo in 1994. It started as "Jerry and David's Guide to the World Wide Web". It was a directory of websites. Each site was organized in hierarchy based on categories and sub-categories. As it expanded, it added a web portal and search. By 1998, Yahoo! was the most popular website on the internet with 30 million unique users per month.[3] Until the dot com implosion in 2000, Yahoo! enjoyed darling status on Wall Street. Its stock peaked at $118.75, but by 2001 had plummeted to $8.11.[4]

The company struggled under a number of CEOs after the crash: Terry Semel from Warner Brothers, Jerry Yang, who returned as interim CEO, Carol Bartz of Autodesk, Scott Thompson of PayPal, and interim CEO Ross Levinsohn. In 2012, having continued to struggle to regain its market position, Yahoo! recruited Marissa Mayer, Product Executive at Google, to turn the company and especially its products around. It was a tall order. Although still in the Fortune 500 at 483, the company's revenue was down 21% from the prior year.[5] Google, one of Yahoo!'s major competitors, was now larger, with over seven times more revenue, and was outspending Yahoo! five to one in research and development.

Mayer went to work trying to rebuild Yahoo!'s business and gain traction in growth markets. By 2016, she had added $1.6 billion in new revenue streams across four growth markets: mobile, video, native search, and social. She focused the company on three platforms: mail, search, and Tumblr (which Yahoo! acquired in 2013 for $1.1 billion). Mayer also sunset 120 legacy products and reduced the workforce by 42%.[6] Even with all of Mayer's efforts, Yahoo! was losing sales from its traditional business lines just as quickly as new revenue was being added. She was pressured by the board to negotiate the sale of the company.

Now let's go back to the period from 2002 to 2006, when Terry Semel was at the reins, to try to understand how Yahoo! got itself into the situation that Mayer was ultimately hired to turnaround. In 2002, Yahoo! had a gap in its product

---

3 http://news.bbc.co.uk/2/hi/business/107667.stm
4 https://en.wikipedia.org/wiki/History_of_Yahoo!
5 http://fortune.com/fortune500/2012/
6 Yahoo Inc 2015 10-K filing

technology. Search on their site was then being provided by a four-year-old company named Google. Yahoo! feared Google was going to challenge them in their core portal business. To prevent this, Yahoo! made a bid for the company, but Google's founders did not want to sell. Semel thought Yahoo!'s $3 billion bid was more than generous and ended the discussions. As much as Semel needed a winning strategy for search, he was not willing to spend the $5 billion it would likely have taken to close the deal. Further, at that price, it would have been more a merger of equals, which Semel could not stomach. Yahoo! finally settled for combining the technologies of Inktomi and Overture. Inktomi had been acquired for $235 million in 2002 for its search technology, and Overture for $1.65 billion in 2003 for its advertising engine. Although the core technology was there, Yahoo! was not able to evolve it fast enough to catch up with Google. By 2006, Google commanded 70% of the fast-growing search-related advertising market.[7]

As Google became synonymous with search, Yahoo! made a play for the social networking site Facebook. It was 2006, and Facebook was just two years old. Like Google's founders, Facebook founder Mark Zuckerberg did not want to sell. Yahoo! finally offered $1 billion and was turned down. It is rumored that had Yahoo! increased its offer to $1.1 billion, the board would have forced the sale. Semel would not increase his bid.[8] Yahoo! made no meaningful progress in social.

Google, during the same time period of 2002–2006, made three significant acquisitions. The first was Applied Semantics for $102 million in 2003. Although this may seem a small amount for the product that became the billion-dollar Adsense business, it was Google's largest acquisition to date. In 2005, seeing consumers shift to mobile, Google purchased Android for an estimated $50 million. It then executed on it with great success, turning it into a true rival of Apple's iOS. Lastly, in 2006 Google secured its place in online video with the purchase of YouTube for $1.65 billion.

Google understood the market and technology trends, made investments at the right time and then executed successfully to turn them into dominant businesses. Of the four major trends — search, mobile, video, and social — it is only the last, social, with which Google has struggled to deploy a successful strategy. For Google, getting three out of four right was enough. Yahoo! missed the opportunity or

7   "How Yahoo Blew It" by Fred Vogelstein, Wired Magazine, February 2007.
8   "Yahoo: 9 Reasons for the Internet Icon's Decline" by Cara McGoogan, The Telegraph, 7/26/2016

failed to execute on all of them (FIGURE 1: STRATEGY EXECUTION COMPARISON). Looking at it through a cultural lens, Terry Semel was a highly-regarded leader and dealmaker from Warner Brothers, a major film studio and distributor. He was not a technologist. Although he definitely understood the trends, he underestimated their importance, how quickly the technologies would diffuse, and the winner-take-all dynamic in technology.

MARKETS	YAHOO!	GOOGLE
Search	◑	●
Mobile	○	●
Video	○	●
Social	○	○

Strategy Execution Level ●=High ◑=Med ○=Low

FIGURE INTRO.1: *Strategy execution comparison for key growth markets between 2002–2006*

In this light, Marissa Mayer was tasked with undoing strategic mistakes that occurred six to ten years before her appointment at Yahoo!. It was a tall order — too tall, in fact. Although she got Yahoo! back into the key growth markets it had missed, she was playing catch-up from the start in all of them, with fewer resources and a weaker position than Google and Facebook.

There is a lot to learn from Yahoo!'s story. Yahoo! made major missteps at the corporate level of strategy. Major acquisitions failed to materialize at Yahoo! between 2002–2006, and its own products did not fill the gap. Although Yahoo! adopted Agile methods in 2005[9] and had everything going for it during the dotcom

9   "Rolling out Agile in a Large Enterprise" by Gabrielle Benefield

era, it was unable to migrate its products into the Web 2.0 world. Furthermore, its flagship products, such as mail, maps, and groups, stagnated and became followers rather than leaders in their markets.

The tale of Yahoo! demonstrates the crucial interplay between corporate strategy, product strategy, and Agile product planning. Most strategy happens at a longer interval than a typical six- to nine-month Agile product plan. Agile is about maximizing the short-term. Strategy is about positioning ourselves where the most value will be in the long-term. Agile enables us to respond quickly to changing market conditions and adjust plans to seize emergent opportunities and/or react to competitors. Strategy lets us know whether, how, and when we should respond. To succeed, Agile product planning must sit on top a foundation of proper strategic planning that sets the right targets and critically evaluates when to rethink those targets. For this reason, strategic planning needs to be treated as a distinct process from Agile product planning, with its own time horizons and purpose.

In the end, Agile development and planning could not save Yahoo! from its strategic choices. And by the time Mayer arrived, neither could she. Yahoo! has not regained its preeminence in the market and, at the time of writing, looks like it never will.

Measuring Success

As product managers, we rarely have perfect data and must fill in the gaps by using our judgement. Understanding whether our strategy is both working and durable is difficult. Given that a strategy may take years to realize, it can be challenging to assess its effectiveness, especially in the early and middle periods of its execution. Benchmarking against the market and peer companies is one way to gauge our strategy as it is being implemented. Some measures worth tracking include:

1. Revenue growth relative to the market growth
2. Unit market share
3. Margins compared to your peer group

Good signs that your strategy is working are your revenues growing faster than the market, your market share expanding, or your average margins surpassing the industry average. Of the three measures listed above, the one that you select should be determined based on your strategy. For example, Google's growing share of online ad spend was an accurate indication that its strategy in search was working and Yahoo!'s was not. Unit market share works well to benchmark products that are bundled or free, such as Android OS vs Apple's iOS or Chrome browser vs. Microsoft's Internet Explorer. In medical equipment and devices, Medtronic's profit margin, for example, has averaged 17% over the past five years compared to Stryker's 12%, while Boston Scientific's dropped to 11%. More impressively, Intuitive Surgical, which has a narrower focus, has enjoyed profit margins of 26% over the same time period (we'll learn about Intuitive Surgical's pricing strategy in Chapter 11: Pricing for Competitive Advantage).

The point behind relative measures versus absolute measures is that growth in itself does not equate to an effective strategy. For example, if your market is growing at 10% and your business is growing at 5% then you are losing relative to your competitors. Improving on your own performance isn't enough. You need to be growing faster than your peers. In addition to assessing the effectiveness of your strategy, you also need to evaluate whether your gains against your benchmarks are accelerating or slowing down. Are you pulling away from your competitors or are they closing the gap? Even if you appear to be winning in your market, you can never relax. Conditions can change, growth markets can saturate, and a new technology can make yours obsolete.

Wrap-up

Given the story of Yahoo!, it is worth considering whether a company can ever come back once it has fallen behind. Turnarounds are difficult. So difficult, in fact, that among companies that experience a significant downturn in revenue growth, only 12% ever return to high growth.[10] One company that did was Apple. The turnaround was led by Steve Jobs when, in 1997, he retook the helm of the company he had founded nearly 20 years earlier. Apple was close to failure, and Jobs had to negotiate a $150 million-dollar investment from Microsoft with his rival Bill Gates to survive. Jobs refocused the company on building great products by introducing the all-in-one iMac. Then, instead of chasing markets Apple had

10 Matthew S. Olson and Derek van Bever, *Stall Points* (Yale University Press, New Haven and London, 2008), Kindle Loc 446

missed, he set out to transform markets with a string of hits including the iPod, iPhone and iPad product lines. Apple beautifully aligned corporate strategy, product strategy, and execution. It was one of the most impressive corporate comebacks in history.

This book is about the art and discipline of strategy. It is intended to guide you in leading your team and product to success. The advice should work whether you are number one in your market or coming from behind. The information is structured in three major sections. *Part 1: Being Strategic* steps you through how to create a product strategy, a vision, a strategic roadmap, and a prioritized product backlog. *Part II: Driving Business Success* provides a framework for evaluating different product-market fit types, evaluating risk, and locating the most promising areas for growth. Lastly, *Part III: Finding Competitive Advantage* covers how to breakdown industries, map a market, and anticipate trends. Collectively, the three sections should provide you with the analytic frameworks for formulating a strategy and committing resources to action.

I have often been asked if I would rather work for a company with a great strategy and poor execution or a poor strategy and great execution. The truth is you need both. But if your company cannot execute, the best strategy in the world will not save you. In Part I, we cover creating realistic plans. Your strategy happens within the context of your company and the resources you can bring to bear. As you read this book, your job is to craft the right strategy for your products, your team, your company, and your unique situation.

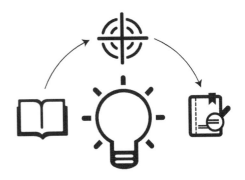

PART I

Being Strategic

To go from idea to successful product, a product needs a strategy, a vision, a roadmap, and a backlog. Strategy sits at the center, binding the other three into a coherent product plan (FIGURE 1.1). The vision inspires the team towards a better future. The roadmap shows how the vision will be achieved over time. The product backlog describes how the roadmap increment is realized. All of them are supported by the product strategy. The strategy ensures the vision is achievable, the roadmap priorities and timing are justified, and the backlog is ordered to deliver optimal value to the customer and the business. The strategy also extends beyond the product, ensuring essential functions such as Marketing, Sales, Distribution and Support understand their roles and are prepared to fulfil them.

FIGURE 1.1: *Product strategy unifies the vision, roadmap and backlog*

One thing that will make discussing product strategy, vision, and roadmap somewhat challenging over the next four chapters is that I don't know your precise relationship to those three topics in the context of your organization. You may be responsible for one or all of them, or you may only influence them, or your role may involve some combination of responsibility and influence over them. As you read these chapters, realize your context matters. If you work in a start-up, the company and product are likely one in the same. Your vision and potentially even the product strategy may come from the founders. In a larger company, with a product manager working alongside a product owner, the vision, product strategy and roadmap likely originate from the product manager with input from the product owner. If you manage a component of a larger solution (say site search for an e-commerce company), your vision, strategy, and road-map will be directly influenced by the product manager's vision, strategy, and roadmap for the entire site, but you will also have your own vision, strategy, and roadmap. Regardless of how these items come into being, as a product manager or a product owner, you need to understand what a solid vision, strategy, and roadmap look like, how to use them, and how to create them.

Part I covers how to create a defensible strategy that combines a high-level vision, a roadmap and prioritized product backlog. Through these activities, you will establish yourself as a strategic product leader in your organization. This section of the book includes the following:

» Chapter 1: Product Strategy
» Chapter 2: Vision
» Chapter 3: Strategic Roadmap
» Chapter 4: Prioritizing the Product Backlog

CHAPTER 1

Product Strategy

Your product strategy unifies your product vision, roadmap and backlog. It also defines how your product will compete in the market. It covers areas such as customer segments, the dimensions of the product most relevant to those customer segments, its competitive differentiation, pricing, distribution, and promotion. Companies have leveraged one or more of these areas to lead their markets for many years or to achieve a successful exit. For example,

1   Apple has long differentiated on design and user experience.

2   Amazon, as we will see in Chapter 2 on vision, is committed to low prices, broad selection, and convenience.

3   Dell dominated the PC era with its direct sales model. The company's service was differentiated but its product was not.

4   Salesforce.com used subscription pricing and a hosted solution to differentiate from installed customer relationship management (CRM) systems that required large upfront license fees and an IT department to install and maintain. Its product features were not unique.

5   Hotmail, the free webmail services that launched in 1996, was an early proof point for viral marketing. When a Hotmail user sent an email using the service, Hotmail appended the text "Get your free email at Hotmail" beneath the sender's signature.[11] Thus, Hotmail used its users

---

11   https://techcrunch.com/2009/10/18/ps-i-love-you-get-your-free-email-at-hotmail/

to promote the service and its unique selling proposition of being free. Hotmail reached 12 million subscribers in two years and was acquired by Microsoft for $400M.[12] Many companies thereafter, including Facebook, used viral marketing to promote their services to acquire new users cost-effectively at unprecedented speed.

1.1 Developing a Product Strategy

There are five elements needed to develop your product strategy (FIGURE 1.2): customer, market, competition, technology, and business strategy. Collecting and analyzing the information from these five areas requires a lot of work. However, mastering this information allows you to formulate your product strategy, inform your vision, develop your product roadmap and prioritize the product backlog. It also helps you defend your prioritization to stakeholders and establish your credibility as the trusted expert who deserves to be guiding the product.

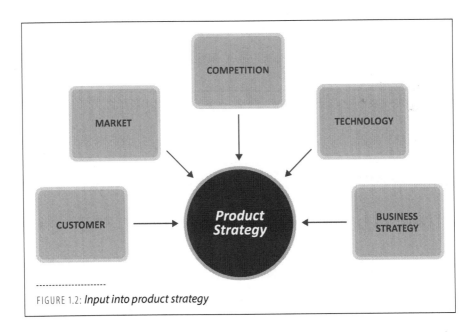

FIGURE 1.2: *Input into product strategy*

---

12 https://en.wikipedia.org/wiki/Outlook.com

Let's look at each element in turn.

1. Customer

 GOAL: Understand the customer's problem and identify opportunities to address it that your competition may not see.

Voice of Customer or VOC research is essential for developing an understanding of the customer. VOC research spans a number of techniques to understand customers' explicit and latent needs and their priorities. This includes a combination of qualitative research and quantitative methods. You should regularly be speaking with your customers to understand their challenges in accomplishing their goals. Observe them using their current solution or your product in the course of their day and identify places where you may be able to better meet their need. Analyze your customer interviews and observations for common themes. This phase of the research focuses on uncovering the breadth of needs and views that customers possess.[13] With that information in hand, you can further survey a larger and even statistically significant set of customers to understand how prevalent each need is and how important solving that need is to your market. You should also review support cases, web analytics (especially usage data) and CRM data if these are available for your type of product.

CASE STUDY: In 2004, I was working for a company developing supply chain solutions for the food service industry. The customers I worked with were major restaurant chains in the fast food and casual dining sectors. This was also the year of a major mad cow disease scare. Consumer behavior changed overnight. Hamburger sales plummeted while chicken sandwich sales skyrocketed. This rapid change in consumer preference wreaked havoc in the supply chain, especially for limited time offers (LTOs), a category of product that was already difficult to manage under ideal conditions. LTOs are the specialty items that restaurant chains make available for a few months at a time, such as a bacon ranch chicken sandwich, and are not part of the permanent menu. By speaking with our purchasing manager customers, we recognized that the technology platform

---

13 In their book *Voices into Choices: Acting on the Voice of the Customer,* authors Gary Burchill and Christina Hepner Brodie advise that 95% of useful information comes from 15–20 well-selected interviews. This would include lead, happy, dissatisfied, former, and non-users. You will also want to include buyers, influencers, and gatekeepers, as well as other relevant segments.

we developed for collecting and analyzing restaurant purchase data could also be used to collect inventory data. The solution would dramatically improve the accuracy and completeness of LTO inventory data for decision guidance. This would allow our customers to avoid shortages and overstocks in their supply chain. Because we were close to our customers in understanding their problems, we were able to be first to market with this novel and timely solution.

2. Market

GOAL: Understand which markets and segments are most important to your product vision. Also, understand where the market is going and forecast the environment and customer expectations when the product is released.

Markets are dynamic and ever-changing. Research the market size, the stage it has reached in its lifecycle, and its growth rate. Drill into the segments of the market and understand how needs, behaviors, and values vary across each one. Prioritize each segment to your product and business and decide for which segments you will optimize. Analyze the value chain, looking for opportunities to consolidate or rethink value delivery. Evaluate the external factors that influence your market. How will demographic shifts or changes in attitudes affect it? What is the legal, regulatory, and legislative landscape and how do you accommodate these risks in your product plan? How do other industries, such as energy, affect your product or the cost of producing, transporting, or delivering it? Are there political risks in regions in which you, your partners, or your suppliers operate?

CASE STUDY: In 2005, Google had built a $6 billion advertising business largely based on desktop search. Nevertheless, Google was worried. Mobile browsing was growing fast and in developing countries consumers were skipping desktop computer adoption altogether — their primary and sometimes only connection to the internet was through their phones. Because of the evolving technology landscape, consumer behavior was changing and changing fast. Google recognized the desktop search market was maturing, and it needed a strategy to become relevant in the mobile world. In response to these market shifts, Google made a bold move and purchased the Android Mobile Operating System.[14] It

---

14 https://en.wikipedia.org/wiki/Android_(operating_system)

then worked to establish it as a dominant platform for smartphones and tablets. By 2016, Google's earned more advertising revenue from mobile than desktop.[15]

3. Competition

GOAL: You need to drive you own product strategy and avoid the trap of following your competitors in the market. If you understand their intent, though, you can anticipate their future moves and predict their reactions to *your* moves. Use this information, along with your VOC customer research, to develop a plan to achieve durable differentiation[16] for your product and define the competitive context.

Customers buy "whole products" based on overall benefits and not just features (FIGURE 1.3). So although feature comparisons are an important aspect of competitive analysis that product managers perform, they show only one small piece of the competitive picture. Map out the whole product to gain a fuller understanding of how competitors stack-up and identify non-feature areas, such as services, in which you can extend your differentiation.

Understand how competitors perform for market share and growth. Is the product area core to their business and will they defend their position vigorously, or is their interest purely opportunistic? Understand how your cost and distribution structure differs from your competitors. Understand not just your competitors' product strategies but also their business strategies. Look for advantages that you can exploit, and identify your own disadvantages — you'll need to guard against them. Lastly, understand the intellectual property landscape (*e.g.* patents, trademarks, and trade secrets) and how it restricts or supports your ability to operate.

CASE STUDY: Founded in 1998 and launched in 1999, Netflix offered the exact same product — a movie rental — as its well-established bricks and mortar competitor Blockbuster LLC. Netflix's business model, however, differentiated the company, giving it a sustained advantage. Netflix used a new technology, the internet, to offer DVD rentals through the mail on a subscription basis. When a customer wanted to watch a new movie, they mailed back

---

15   "Mobile Moves to Majority Share of Google's Worldwide Ad Revenues", eMarketer, October 24, 2016
16   Durable differentiation allows you to compete on value versus price.

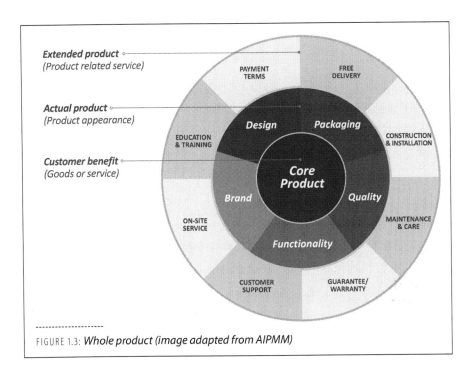

FIGURE 1.3: *Whole product (image adapted from AIPMM)*

the last DVD Netflix had sent them, and Netflix would send the next DVD in the customer's queue. With Blockbuster, customers had to go to the store, rent a DVD and then return it within a short rental window of one to five days based on the popularity of the movie.

Netflix's business model had two major advantages over Blockbuster's. The first was convenience. The movies showed up at the customer's door. The second was no late fees. Late fees were a major source of dissatisfaction among Blockbuster's customers, but those fees were also an important component of the company's revenue. Late fees earned Blockbuster $800 million in the year 2000[17] and management could not easily do away with them. As a result, Netflix enjoyed six years of differentiation in the market on just this single customer delighter. By the time Blockbuster finally relented and switched to a "no late fees" policy in 2005, it was already in irreversible decline.[18] Furthermore, Netflix used those six years from its

---

17 In 2000, late fees accounted for 16% of Blockbuster's revenue, earning them nearly $800 million. http://www.nbcnews.com/id/39332696/ns/business-retail/t/hubris-late-fees-doomed-blockbuster/
18 http://www.fastcompany.com/1690654/blockbuster-bankruptcy-decade-decline

launch to refine its website and recommendations engine, mitigating Blockbuster's major advantage — the ease of discovering movies on the store shelf.[19]

With Blockbuster eliminated as a threat and broadband internet becoming widely available, Netflix's strategy needed a refresh. The company chose to transition to streaming video content. It required a huge investment that would ultimately cannibalize its own DVD rental business.[20] Netflix, however, lacked a durable differentiator in the streaming space even with its lauded recommendations technology. To address this issue, the company developed original, exclusive content. At the time of writing, it is too early to know if Netflix will retain its dominant position in the video streaming market, but we can appreciate how the company proactively evolved its product strategy and offering to differentiate itself in intensely competitive markets.

4. Technology

 GOAL: Understand how technology will impact your market and your ability to solve your customers' problems.

Technology often creates new ways to solve problems that were not formerly feasible, or ways to address problems at a lower cost than previously, making your solutions available to an underserved customer segment. Just as you would forecast where the market will be when your product is released, you also need to forecast where *technology* will be, and incorporate this forecast into your decision making and priorities. This includes new and emerging technology standards that are relevant to your industry (such as XML, TCP, IEEE 802.3U). The three main technology dimensions to explore are i) capabilities, ii) adoption rates, and iii) costs. The first influences what's possible, the second affects the size of the market, and the third the competitiveness and accessibility of your product.

---

19   Netflix launched with a la carte DVD rentals and sales. It was only after extensive market research, and a desperate need to find a path to profitability, that the Netflix team validated the subscription model. The recommendation engine was initially created out of the necessity to steer customers away from the new releases and towards less known content that they would enjoy. Netflix's research also showed that retention was much higher when DVDs arrived the next day (a whole product consideration). They spent considerable effort positioning distribution centers in major markets. For more on Netflix's story, read the 2012 book, *Netflixed* by Gina Keating.
20   Netflix first started streaming content in 2007

CASE STUDY: In the late 80s, pen-based tablet computing was touted as the next big thing. A number of companies pursued it, including Apple (with their Newton project); Jerry Kaplan's high-flying startup, GO Corporation;[21] and Microsoft. In the end, the technology just wasn't there. Newton was cancelled after five disappointing years, GO was acquired by AT&T in a distress sale, and Microsoft's Windows for Pen computing and subsequent attempts failed to gain widespread traction.[22] These companies all misread the technology trends.

Contrast this with Apple's introduction of the iPhone and iPad in 2007 and 2010 respectively. Apple had re-approached the problem. Instead of scaling down a computer, they scaled up a mobile phone — a product category where compactness, low cost, and energy efficiency were all prized attributes. Through phones, the technology had finally arrived to allow both the iPhone and iPad to push the bounds of what was technically possible in a form factor and at a price point that made them attractive to consumers. Apple then executed beautifully with an elegant, intuitive, and functional interface. Furthermore, digital cellular and home wireless networks, critical enablers for these two products, were already in place, facilitating wide-scale adoption.[23] In the first quarter of 2017, the sales of iPhone and iPads comprised 76% of Apple's total revenue.[24]

5. Business Strategy

GOAL: Understand how your product fits into and supports your company's strategy. Evaluate your company's competencies.

Your company should have a strategic plan determined by executive management and approved by the board of directors. Your product needs to be part of, and fit into, this plan. Your product may enable your company to grow in a new market, stay competitive in an existing market, or throw off cash to invest in other areas of the business. The role your product plays for the company will impact how you manage it. This is also true if you are responsible for a component of a larger product. In this case, your part of the solution needs to support the larger product strategy, which in turn supports the business strategy.

---

21   Mr. Kaplan shared his experience in his 1999 book *Startup: a Silicon Valley adventure.*
22   http://usatoday30.usatoday.com/tech/news/story/2012-06-19/microsoft-tablet-history/55682538/1
23   For a framework on analyzing ecosystem readiness for a new technology, consult "Right Tech, Wrong Time" by Ron Adner and Rahul Kapoor, HBR article, November 2016.
24   https://www.statista.com/statistics/382260/segments-share-revenue-of-apple/

You also need to evaluate your choice of strategy relative to the company's capabilities and culture. The safest option is to leverage your company's existing competencies. Sometimes, however, a change is necessary. For example, if your company has dedicated account managers and supports a high level of customization of its products, it will require a cultural shift and new skills to succeed in a high volume, low margin segment of the market. If you wanted to take your product in that direction, your plan needs to include how to bring on the new capabilities and develop the systems to successfully support the product.

CASE STUDY: One startup I joined had just gone through a major round of layoffs the previous week. Management tasked me with bringing a new product to market on an extremely tight schedule with a small team. Delivering on time meant meeting our contractual commitment with three major customers and allowing the company to book all-important revenue. Retaining these key customers and realizing the revenue (and much-needed cash) from having the product in the market were critical to the company's strategy for growth through expansion of its offerings with current clients.

Knowing the result my product had to deliver for my company allowed me to make tough trade-offs to ensure the product i) released on time in its smallest form possible and ii) still met our customers' needs. Missing either objective would have meant failure. The release was not the product I wanted to build. If I'd had the luxury of another sixty days, I would have chosen to hold the release to resolve a major deficiency in the design. But it was the product I needed to build so I would have a second chance, with a version two, to release the product I envisioned. Your product strategy must incorporate the business outcome your product needs to fulfill for your company and the time horizon to meet that objective.

Wrap-up

In summary, understanding your customer, the market, your competition, the technology, and your company's strategy are critical inputs to your product strategy and ultimately the prioritization equation. It is this knowledge that allows you to understand your customers' most pressing unmet needs, the highest value segment of the market on which to focus given your strengths, and therefore the minimum viable product to release to that market segment. Knowing the customers' needs and how your competitors think allows you to identify gaps in the market that you can capture and own. Lastly, understanding how your product fits into your company's business strategy allows you to position your product in the right way to secure the resources and support you need from management to deliver on your product plan.

CHAPTER 2

Vision

The product vision is your product's *raison d'etre*. It is a high-level articulation that communicates the product's value, often by painting a picture of the future. A well-expressed vision gives your team everyday benefits by providing context for decision making and alignment around a common goal.

Visions range from practical statements to lofty ambitions. But regardless of where they are on the spectrum of practical to lofty, visions should be concise, inspiring, and an expression of the future state of the world. The vision should state the *who*, *why* and *what* and sometimes the *how*. This translates to the customer (*who*), the problem solved by the solution (*why*), and the attributes that set the product apart, such as feature, price, service, place (*what* and *how*).

The Best Product Pitch Ever

One of the best product pitches and visions I have ever listened to is President John F. Kennedy's 1961 speech to Congress to accelerate funding for the space program.[25] He wanted a colossal amount of money to pursue a project with undefined benefits, and he succeeded in getting it. Kennedy timed the speech well. It came shortly after the US had put its first astronaut, Alan Shepard, into orbit but was still playing catch-up to the Soviet Union in the space race. Kennedy states his vision in one sentence:

I believe that this nation should commit itself to achieving the goal, before this decade is out, of landing a man on the moon and returning him safely to the earth.

The success criteria are so easy to understand:

1. Put someone on the moon
2. Return him safely to earth
3. Do it by the end of the decade (about 9 years)

Kennedy starts the speech with the "why" of the United States.

These are extraordinary times. And we face an extraordinary challenge. Our strength as well as our convictions have imposed upon this nation the role of leader in freedom's cause.

He introduces the market context and establishes a sense of urgency: the Soviet Union poses a competitive threat — an existential threat, in fact — with their lead in space exploration. Nations and citizens of the world have a choice: brand USA or brand Soviet Union. Leadership in space matters to that choice.

If we are to win the battle that is now going on around the world between freedom and tyranny, the dramatic achievements in space which occurred in recent weeks should have made clear to us all, as did the Sputnik in 1957, the impact of this adventure on the minds of men everywhere, who are attempting to make a determination of which road they should take.

25 https://www.presentationmagazine.com/president-kennedy-speech-man-on-the-moon-7508.htm

Kennedy goes on to discuss the budget he needs. He is specific how the funds will be used to create a lunar lander, rocket boosters, and projects beyond the immediate goal of landing a man on the moon. Kennedy even employs a technique adopted by Lean known as *set-based development* when he announces that the project is going to pursue two designs in parallel, in order to mitigate risk and to learn:

> *We propose to develop alternate liquid and solid fuel boosters, much larger than any now being developed, until certain which is superior.*

Kennedy states that he is asking for a firm commitment from Congress (which is responsible for appropriating the budget). He is upfront that the project will last many years and carry a heavy cost. Although his 10-year vision contains clear metrics of success, he tells Congress the actual benefit is unknown.

> *It is a most important decision that we make as a nation... and no one can predict with certainty what the ultimate meaning will be of mastery of space.*

A little over a year later, Kennedy delivered his more famous "We Choose to Go to the Moon" speech that was held outdoors, on a hot day, in the football stadium at Rice University, Texas. Unlike the budget request the previous year, this speech was a sales pitch to the public. The President masterfully frames hard to understand technical facts and mission details in the context of football fields, mechanical watches, and the local weather.[26]

> *We shall send to the moon, 240,000 miles away from the control station in Houston, a giant rocket more than 300 feet tall, the length of this football field, made of new metal alloys, some of which have not yet been invented, capable of standing heat and stresses several times more than have ever been experienced, fitted together with a precision better than the finest watch, carrying all the equipment needed for propulsion, guidance, control, communications, food and survival, on an untried mission, to an unknown celestial body, and then return it safely to earth, re-entering the atmosphere at speeds of over 25,000 miles per hour, causing heat about half that of the temperature of the sun — almost as hot as it is here today — and do all this, and do it right, and do it first before this decade is out — then we must be bold.*

He even makes large budget numbers accessible to his audience:

---

26   http://er.jsc.nasa.gov/seh/ricetalk.htm

> *To be sure, all this costs us all a good deal of money. This year's space budget is three times what it was in January 1961, and it is greater than the space budget of the previous eight years combined. That budget now stands at $5,400 million a year — a staggering sum, though somewhat less than we pay for cigarettes and cigars every year.*

There is much we as product managers can learn on selling our products and vision from John F. Kennedy. Kennedy reminds us of the "why" and provides context for the decisions. He states a clear objective of success and the time frame. Then he simply describes the pieces of the solution and how the money will be spent. Lastly, he takes hard to grasp technical detail and numbers and relates them to familiar objects and situations.■

2.1 Toyota's Lofty Vision

Toyota President, Katsuaki Watanabe, shared his vision of the future for his company's cars in a 2007 Harvard Business Review article:[27]

> *I don't know how many years it's going to take us, but I want Toyota to come up with the dream car — a vehicle that can make the air cleaner than it is, a vehicle that cannot injure people, a vehicle that prevents accidents from happening, a vehicle that can make people healthier the longer they drive it, a vehicle that can excite, entertain, and evoke the emotions of its occupants, a vehicle that can drive around the world on just one tank of gas.*

This is a lofty vision. It tackles challenging and sometimes opposing priorities of safety, energy use, environmental impact, and the experience of the driver and passengers. One can imagine how the team that developed Toyota's highly successful Prius hybrid, the first mass-produced hybrid vehicle in the world, internalized this vision.

---

27   https://hbr.org/2007/07/lessons-from-toyotas-long-drive

2.2 Spotify's Broad Vision

Spotify, the Swedish music streaming company, has a broad yet more practical vision than Toyota: *give people access to all the music they want, all the time, in a completely legal and accessible way.*[28] The vision is open ended. Defining one's target segment as "people" is usually too general. Yet this word choice makes one thing clear: Spotify is an advocate for the consumer, not for the artist. It may be no surprise that the company has clashed with artists and record labels over royalty fees for the music that it streams. Musician Taylor Swift even removed her songs from Spotify in 2014.[29] Most interesting for me about Spotify's vision is that the company specifies that the product must work in a completely legal way. Usually complying with the law is just a given, but with the history of digital piracy and illegal peer-to-peer sharing sites in the music industry, it does merit being called out.

There are times when companies deliberately choose to test the bounds of the law. The now-defunct music sharing site Napster did this unsuccessfully. Ride-sharing service Uber, however, has carefully worked in the gray area of the law by classifying its drivers as independent contractors and claiming exemption from regulations that cover taxi services. At the time of writing, Uber has been relatively successful at defending its position.

2.3 Amazon's Practical Vision

At their most practical, vision statements turn into product positioning statements. In his seminal, high-technology marketing book *Crossing the Chasm* published in 1991, author Geoffrey Moore defines the structure of the positioning statement as:

> For [target customer] who [statement of the need or opportunity] the [product name] is a [product category] that [statement of key benefit — that is, compelling reason to buy] Unlike [primary competitive alternative] our product [statement of primary differentiation]

----

28   https://twitter.com/spotify/status/141929408763142144
29   http://time.com/3554468/why-taylor-swift-spotify/

Take a moment to think about the positioning statement for your current product. What did you come up with? If you haven't already done this exercise, you may find it's a lot harder than it looks.

In 2001, when Amazon.com was establishing itself as an online bookstore, its positioning statement was:

> *For World Wide Web users who enjoy books, Amazon.com is a retail bookseller that provides instant access to over one million books. Unlike traditional book retailers, Amazon.com provides a combination of extraordinary convenience, low prices, and comprehensive selection.*[30]

Breaking down Amazon's positioning statement:

1. **WHO** — worldwide web (www) users who enjoy books. For reference, in 2001, only about half the US population was online.[31]

2. **WHY** — instant access to 1.1 million books. This was approximately five times more titles than an average Barnes and Noble retail store[32].

3. **WHAT** — convenience, low prices and comprehensive selection. These three values permeate Amazon to the present day with the company's patented one-click ordering feature, its push to digital publishing and low cost e-readers and tablets, and its expansion into a dizzying array of product categories beyond books.

---

30 http://cultbranding.com/ceo/create-strong-brand-positioning-strategy/

31 http://data.worldbank.org/indicator/IT.NET.USER.P2?view=map&year=2001

32 http://web.archive.org/web/20050208032625/http://www.barnesandnobleinc.com/our_company/our_main_businesses/our_main_businesses.html

When Amazon launched its $199 Kindle Fire tablet, at less than half the price of Apple's dominant iPad, company CEO Jeff Bezos wrote of Amazon's value-based positioning in a letter to customers posted on the company's homepage. Taking a direct swipe at Apple, Bezos wrote: "…there are two types of companies: those that work hard to charge customers more, and those that work hard to charge customers less. Both approaches can work. We are firmly in the second camp."[33] ∎

Wrap-up

Whether your vision is lofty like Toyota's or more practical like Spotify's and Amazon's, it acts as a guidepost for decision making. Unlike the product strategy, which can be complex and involved, the vision is an easy-to-understand articulation of the most important parts of the plan. The vision keeps three crucial factors front and center for the team: i) the target customer; ii) the in-scope problems that the product solves; and iii) the most important dimensions of the product.

Once you have developed your vision, you have to communicate it, and not just once. You have to say it over and over again, until the team and your stakeholders know it and can repeat it, and you are sick of hearing yourself speak. Even then, you should still reiterate the vision from time to time to keep it fresh in everyone's memory.

---

33   Source: https://techcrunch.com/2011/10/02/amazon-punches-apple-hard-with-kindle-fires-199-price/

CHAPTER 3

Strategic Roadmap

With your vision and product strategy in place, the next piece is the strategic roadmap (FIGURE 3.1). The roadmap shows how you will achieve your vision. It tells the story of how your product will evolve over time as you execute on your product strategy, and the business outcome at each phase. As with developing the product strategy, creating a roadmap is a process that requires you to understand the needs of multiple stakeholders. It also may be the first time your vision and strategy will need to explicitly accommodate the constraints of your development resources.

Like so many terms in product management, *roadmap* means different things to different people. In the context of this book, I am discussing a *strategic roadmap*. A strategic roadmap distills your product strategy into sets of capabilities that you want to release in a given sequence over a defined time frame. For each time frame, the roadmap needs to show three things: i) the business outcomes that will be achieved by the product investment over a specified period; ii) the capability set that will be released; and iii) the external market conditions that justify why you are advocating that capability set at that point in time. Strategic roadmaps ultimately answer the questions "why?" and "why now?"

Now, just so there is no confusion, let's look at what a roadmap is not. You do not create a roadmap by taking the product backlog and slicing it into releases based on when you estimate the team will get to each feature, and then listing those features on a timeline by release. A roadmap built in this manner is bottom-up and does not tie to the product strategy. It is a *what* roadmap and neglects to answer the questions of *why* the set of features are important to both the business and customer, and *why* the timing and sequencing make sense. A *what* roadmap is likely to be sidetracked based on the crisis of the month and throw you back into chasing the market versus leading the market.

3.1 Step 1 — Lay out the External Environment

Start the roadmapping process by laying out along a timeline the external market environment in which your product competes. The relevant external factors will vary by product and market. Expect to have three to five swim lanes for external categories covering a timeline of about three years. The shortest I would recommend is 18 months and the longest is five years. Common categories that may pertain to your products include:

1. **TECHNOLOGY** — include adoption within the market or your customer base, cost curves that indicate when the technology is viable for inclusion in your solution, capabilities that you can exploit, such as network speed, and standards that you need or want to support.

2. **REGULATORY** — requirements or non-technology standards that your product needs to support. In the healthcare market, the International Statistical Classification of Diseases and Related Health Problems (ICD) is a list of codes used in medical records to categorize, invoice, and report on diseases, symptoms, complaints and more. At the time of writing, health systems are switching from ICD-9 to ICD-10 and vendors are adapting their systems to the new standard. Similarly, companies working on autonomous vehicles need to comply with regulations that vary by state, making that market challenging.

3. **MARKET TRENDS** (by segment) — plot the trends affecting a market or a market segment. The launch of Apple's iPhone kicked off a work trend known as BYOD (bring your own device) to which businesses had to adjust. It typically affected many groups within a company: IT and security groups had to ensure corporate data remained secure, while HR and legal teams needed to define policy, enforce compliance and

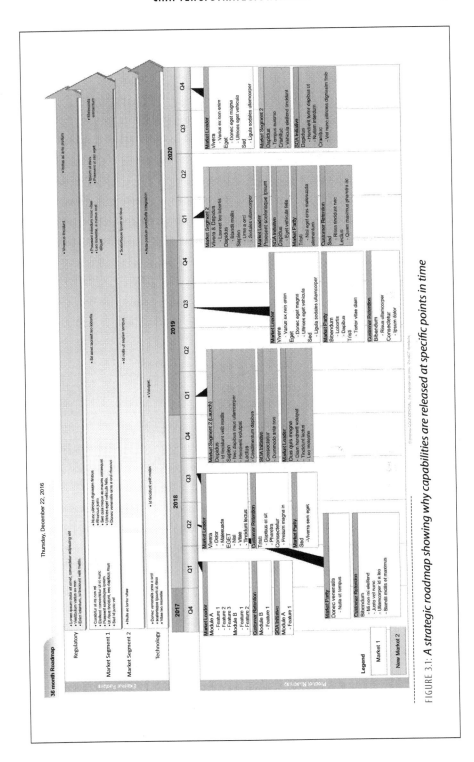

FIGURE 3.1: *A strategic roadmap showing why capabilities are released at specific points in time*

address issues regarding employee privacy and appropriate use.[34] If you developed products to help these groups do their job, BYOD was a trend you needed to track and incorporate into your roadmap. When plotting adoption over time, think in terms of early adopter, early majority, late majority, and laggards — and the point along the curve that you need to have a product available.

4   **COMPETITORS** — list major product releases or capabilities anticipated by key competitors that will affect your competitiveness in the market, delay purchase decisions, provide negotiating leverage with customers, or create FUD (fear, uncertainty, and doubt) in the marketplace.

5   **TRADE OR SEASONAL EVENTS** — some businesses are event- or season-driven. Personal tax software has to be out by end-of-year, and accountants I have spoken with will not touch their accounting software between January and April 15th when personal taxes are due. This business lives and dies on the tax season and annual changes to tax law. In other industries, companies use major trade events to launch products. Electronic Entertainment Expo or E3 has played this role for gaming companies since 1995.

6   **CUSTOMER COMMITMENTS** — these are contractual obligations you have made to your customers to deliver a product on a given date. They are similar to events, in that they represent a deadline that must be met. However, they differ from events in that the commitment may be renegotiable or at least forgiving of small delays, whereas tax season and trade shows happen whether your product is ready or not.

3.2 Step 2 — Add your Product Plan and Strategic Objectives

Once you have framed the external factors, start placing key releases on the timeline, along with and the strategic objectives they fulfil, and under that the key product capabilities that are critical to that release.

---

34   http://www.govinfosecurity.com/webinars/mobile-learn-from-intels-cisos-on-securing-employee-owned-devices-w-264

The objectives will vary by your context. General objectives may include categories such as Market Leadership, Market Parity, Customer Retention, Customer Acquisition, or New Market. The objectives may be more measurable and tie to defined business outcomes (see Chapter 4, section 4.2: Define Value Based on Desired Outcome). They can also tie to internal initiatives, such as platform rationalization. Once, not long ago, an objective for many companies was creating a mobile solution as the world adopted smartphones. For enterprise products, a release may also be tied to a specific customer.

If your organization releases in regular cycles, the spacing of releases across the roadmap will be at regular intervals. Likewise, if you work in a continuous or close to continuous deployment environment, it is not reasonable to list each deployment. Rather, list the primary objectives that will be met and the matching capabilities that will be released each quarter.

3.3 Vetting with Development, Dependencies and Resource Constraints

Development and other stakeholders should be involved in the process of creating the roadmap. Roadmaps need to be built with resource constraints in mind. There always comes a point as you approach the end of the process where you need to step back, call everyone into the room, and ask if the plan is realistic, especially over the first 12-18 months. The questions to ask are: can the team do this amount of work? Have we allowed enough buffer for unplanned work? And have we captured the architectural work that Engineering needs time to complete so they can continue to evolve the solution efficiently?

If you have multiple product lines or complex products, you also need to map out dependencies on shared components of the system and/or on shared teams. Dependencies add complexity to roadmapping and planning, but are a reality that must be accommodated. Loose coupling between components is ideal, but not always possible. Better to identify dependencies upfront and manage them throughout the release cycles than neglect them to the point where you lose operational flexibility. Evaluating dependencies is a critical aspect of developing an achievable roadmap.

During the vetting phase, you may realize you cannot implement your strategy on the time frame your business requires, or that you cannot take full advantage of the market window. In these situations, it is incumbent upon you to put the case for more resources for your product or to recast the plan. If you expect to request more funding, be realistic about the length of the decision cycle to get approval, and the time it will take to scale the team once approved. Scaling a team always takes longer than you expect, whether you are hiring or contracting.

3.4 Presenting your Roadmap

Strategic roadmaps contain a lot of information. I prefer to build them on a wall, with the team using sticky notes or specialized roadmap cards. If your team is distributed and absolutely cannot be brought together for this exercise, online collaboration tools like RealtimeBoard can work, although they are a little clunky because you cannot take in the whole map in a single view. Once the roadmap is complete, transfer it to a 3-foot by 5-foot canvas using Visio or a similar tool.[35] The subsequently printed plots can be hung on a wall so the team and stakeholders can walk through it. The digital PDF is also fairly easy for someone to review on their computer. Putting the final product in Visio and printing it gives it a level of permanence that says to stakeholders that the team has thought deeply about the direction of the product. Although the team remains flexible to changing conditions, it is going to take evidence and a convincing discussion for you to shift your plan.

The one challenge of the strategic roadmap is it absolutely does not compress down to a single, readable PowerPoint (PPT) slide — and sometimes you need to present in PowerPoint. In these instances, break the roadmap out over multiple slides. One product is about all that you can fit on a slide and still maintain readability. These slides still need to convey the objective of each release. You can consolidate multiple products on a slide if you remove the detail of each product to summarize the overall plan. I usually address the external factors in a separate slide that sets the context before I present the product slides, and may keep a single external factor swim lane on the product detail slides.

----
35   There are currently a number of online roadmap applications. None of these explicitly support the external environment swim lanes necessary for strategic roadmapping. I expect they will in the near future.

Wrap-up

In summary, a strategic roadmap is the single view that shows how your product will evolve over time to achieve your vision and effectively address the external market environment in which your product must compete. The roadmap shows the business objective, and thus justification, for each major release. When created in a collaborative process, a strategic roadmap helps focus all stakeholders on the pieces of the product that must be developed to achieve the strategy. Unlike the product vision, and even the product strategy, the roadmap takes into account the resources available to get the job done. In other words, the roadmap has been vetted against the team's capacity to produce a credible plan.

CHAPTER 4

Prioritizing the
Product Backlog

W ith your product vision, product strategy, and roadmap in place, you are ready and have the knowledge you need to effectively prioritize your product backlog. Prioritization, however, is one of the hardest tasks product managers (and product owners) face. You only have so many resources for your product, and your job is to ensure that the highest value work is being planned and taken to market. Prioritization, therefore, is one of the most important ways you can influence the success of your product and achieve competitive advantage in the marketplace. Take the time to become proficient in this skill. This is where you will commit resources to action.

4.1 Assessing Business Value

Product owners have traditionally been taught to prioritize the product backlog by business value. That is what I taught product owners for many years. On the surface this makes sense: one should place the highest value items at the top of the backlog to be completed first. The problem is that although it is simple in principle, prioritizing by business value is really hard in practice.

First, there is no single measure of business value that applies to your product at all phases of its lifecycle, or to which all items in the product backlog can easily be reduced and quantified. Early on, it might be customer acquisition; late in a product's life, it might be maximizing profits.

Second, large jumps in value are often only realized by a collection of features and stories. If you are building an e-commerce site, for example, your solution has no value unless a consumer can find a product *and* buy it. Value is only created when those two capabilities are combined. The capability for merchandise managers to upload products into the catalog, the capability to make the products discoverable by customers, and the capability to allow the customer to pay are each major parts of a working solution. Each is made up of many other, smaller features.

Third, value creation exists within the context of your company. There may be a conflict between what delivers the most value for your company and what is best for your product. At one company I worked for, Marketing kicked-off an initiative to rename the company's individual products to make them more consistent with each other and the value they delivered. The initiative required a meaningful amount of work from each team to update the product name in the user interface and online documentation. This work delayed other features that would have improved the performance of the actual product.

Lastly, your time horizon matters. Is it more important to improve short-term gains or long-term gains for your product or company? In the previous chapter, I shared a story about a startup where I had to get a product out because the company needed the revenue. A few years later at the same company, our product strategy was succeeding and the company was profitable. Product Management and Engineering decided to have all products share a single analytics layer. The objective of the project was to create a more uniform experience for our users while reducing the engineering resources required to maintain that layer of the solution. Migrating the products to the new analytics platform was a significant effort that represented a short-term loss for a long-term gain. It would not have made sense to attempt this when the company was struggling for economic survival.

4.2 Define Value Based on Desired Outcome

Instead of trying to assign a mythical return on investment (ROI) to each item in the backlog, a more practical approach is to define the desired business outcome for the next release or calendar quarter.

Examples:

1 Increase
    a   Revenue, profit, or unit sales
    b   Customer acquisition
    c   Customer satisfaction
    d   Customer retention
    e   Market share
    f   Usage: frequency of use, time spent during a session, number of users within a customer site
    g   Value realization: similar but more specific than usage. Identify the action within your product that generates the value for the user.
2 Reduce
    a   Operational costs
    b   Support volume
3 Neutralize a competitor's advantage
4 Validate a market need

As you can see from the list above, how you think about and measure value depends on what you are trying to achieve for your product. Return on Investment (ROI), even if it could be calculated for each item in the product backlog, may not be the best way to express value. You may want to consider value from the customer perspective. Typical value realization actions for a user are creating a document or sharing that document with another user in the system. For a non-profit crowdfunding application I worked on, value realization didn't occur when the user signed-up to fundraise or even when they got their first donation. It occurred when the user uploaded contacts and sent out their first email through the system. Those were the users who would succeed in achieving an ambitious fundraising goal. Take a moment to review the examples in the list above. What is the single most important objective you want to achieve with the next release of your product?

There is a problem with the above list, however. The language is too vague. Outcomes need to be specific. They should describe the measurement, the target, and the time frame. An example might be to achieve monthly recurring revenue (MRR) of $10 million dollars by the end of the year. With a specific and measurable metric, you can identify sub-metrics that will get you to your objective. For example, you might decide that a good way to achieve your objective would be to increase customer retention, aiming (for example) for a 5% improvement within 90 days of the release. To improve that customer retention metric, you could focus on a value realization metric, such as increasing sharing of documents between users by 20%.

Having a clear and measurable objective helps to frame the backlog prioritization. It also provides leeway for the team to incorporate new learning into subsequent sprints and adjust the plan so you are always maximizing the value of the work the team does. Lastly, these same objectives should be visible in your roadmap (discussed in Chapter 3: Strategic Roadmap) and you should anchor the purpose of each release and capability called out in your plan.

4.3 Lenses of Prioritization

We know our objective and how we're going to measure success. It is now time to lay out the detailed path and steps that the team is going to take to get there by prioritizing the product backlog. This last section of the chapter covers a number of techniques (TABLE 4.1) or what I like to call "lenses" to assist in framing the final prioritization discussion and analysis, especially of the product backlog. The techniques are best applied to prioritizing customer needs and features, but some can also be applied at the product or project level. Each of the methods has its strengths and weaknesses. By applying multiple techniques, you can avoid blind spots in your thinking and develop a nuanced understanding of where you need to focus your product to drive results.

METHOD	STRENGTHS	BLIND SPOTS
ROI (return on investment)	Quickly understood metric for comparing projects, and always an important question to answer for management.	Favors short term financial gain over long term sustainable growth or nascent markets. Not all decisions can be directly tied to an ROI, and it does not map to the product strategy.
VOC (voice of customer)	Provides a good picture of customer pain points and can help you identify latent needs and customer priorities. VOC research is a critical input into other prioritization methods such as WSJF.	You need to know where the market is going, as customers cannot articulate the problems they are not currently experiencing. VOC will not let you know that you need to go after new markets or segments.
MoSCoW (must, should, could, won't)	Clearly expresses current priorities.	Hard to apply correctly and can lead to "me too" products and over investment in low-value areas of the product.
Kano Model	Excels at evaluating your investment from the customers' perspective to ensure a differentiated product.	Does not include cost or product strategy view.
Prioritization Matrix	Explicitly connects the value of a feature to the current product strategy.	Does not include cost and is highly subjective.
WSJF Method (weighted shortest job first)	Well-balanced method that accounts for value, time sensitivity, cost and long vs. short term benefits.	Value not explicitly connected to product strategy or customer perspective.
Time Sensitivity Analysis	Makes explicit how to weight calendar time in the prioritization decision.	Narrow lens that only looks at time as a factor.
Feature Lifecycle	Helps to manage cost and risk by spreading investment across a feature's lifecycle, so learning can be incorporated at each stage.	This is a narrow lens used to slice a feature. It cannot be used to compare features against each other.
VRC Matrix (value, risk, cost)	Perfect for visualizing a portfolio of features, understanding how they contribute to the solution, and balancing your investment across value and risk.	Value not explicitly connected to product strategy or customer perspective. Value and risk assessment are highly subjective.

TABLE 4.1: *Summary of prioritization methods*

4.3.1 ROI

Return on investment or ROI will always be a useful lens to evaluate financial outcomes of projects and the product backlog. It is especially important if you own the business case. ROI can be approached from the perspective of your company (*i.e.* how much your organization will make for its development dollar) or from your customer (*i.e.* how much you can improve their revenues or reduce their costs). Remember, ROI is only as good as the assumptions that go into it. Avoid being lulled into the belief that, because your spreadsheet spits out a number, the answer is necessarily accurate. You can get a better grasp on uncertainty by including scenario, sensitivity, and risk analysis in your ROI calculations.

4.3.2 VOC Research

Your voice of customer (VOC) research findings (discussed in Chapter 1: Product Strategy) is one of the most valuable sources of data and insights for prioritization. You really cannot prioritize effectively if you have not done some level of VOC research. Your research can include in-depth interviews, observations, usability studies, support cases, and surveys, to name a few. Ideally, you have had the opportunity to conduct both qualitative and quantitative research with your customers to understand their needs, priorities, and how well those needs are being met by current solutions. Customer research has been an essential tool in all my projects. It has helped me to optimize value as well as steer clear of disaster. In the previous chapter, I shared a story about a startup where I had to deliver a product to market on an extremely tight schedule. During that project, I devoted considerable hours to VOC research. The knowledge I gained meant I could ruthlessly prioritize that first release to hit the deadline and still preserve the essential capabilities to solve our customers' use case.

4.3.3. MoSCoW Method

The MoSCoW method has been around for many years. It was developed by Dai Clegg and widely used with the Dynamic Systems Development Method (DSDM).

[36] I recall first using the method in the early 2000s. MoSCoW is an acronym that stands for Must Have, Should Have, Could Have, and Won't Have. These classifications refer to the current release. Thus, a release would not be considered done if a Must Have item was missing. Likewise, an item marked Won't Have will not be in the current release but its inclusion in the list means it is something the team would like to include in the future. MoSCoW can be helpful for the first level prioritization of an upcoming release. It will not produce a fully ordered backlog, but will at least give you four buckets in which to group items.

I have personally found MoSCoW difficult to implement. The classification does not give insight into how an item will contribute to the release or the level of effort to apply to that item. Further, there is a tendency to restrict the Must Haves to those items without which the product would not work. From a product management perspective, looking to differentiate in the market, Must Have really needs to mean those items without which the product would not be commercially successful. Thus a feature that is not essential for the operation of the product but does create commercial differentiation may be a Must Have. A framework that I find overcomes the limitations of MoSCoW is the Kano model, which is described next.

4.3.4 Kano Model

Professor Noriaki Kano developed his eponymous model in the 1980s.[37] It looks at how the inclusion or exclusion of a feature contributes to customer satisfaction and how that satisfaction changes based on the level of the implementation (FIGURE 4.1). What emerges are three primary curves: must haves, performance, and delighters.

The Must Have curve includes those items whose absence creates dissatisfaction but whose presence leaves users neutral. Must haves are the features customers expect in the product. For a laptop computer, the trackpad might be considered a must have item. Customers do not get excited when a trackpad accurately reflects their swipes and taps. It is just expected to work. They do, however, get frustrated when the trackpad captures false taps and causes unintended actions.

----

36   https://en.wikipedia.org/wiki/MoSCoW_method
37   https://en.wikipedia.org/wiki/Kano_model

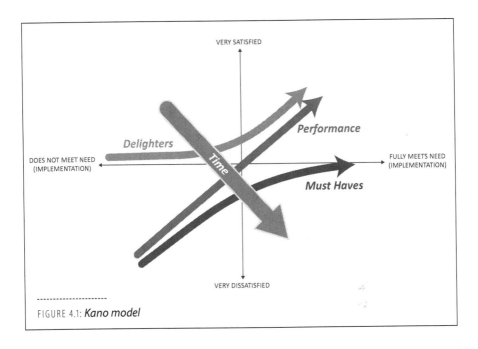

FIGURE 4.1: *Kano model*

Performance items are those that cause the customer dissatisfaction when done poorly and increasing satisfaction when done well. For a laptop computer, battery life sits on the performance curve. Having one's battery not last through a long meeting is frustrating. Having it last all day while working at a customer's site is awesome. Less obvious areas also fall under performance, such as usability or packaging. I encourage digital teams to look at the most mundane aspects of their products, those which we might mistakenly think of as a must have, and treat them as a performance opportunity on which to further differentiate.

The third curve is the delighter. Delighters are items customers do not expect in a product. Thus, their presence can create joy, but their absence leaves the customer with neither positive nor negative feelings. Facial recognition on a laptop for authentication might be considered a delighter. It removes the tedious task of having to type in a password.

When using Kano, I work with the team to map out all the features being considered for the release and determine on which curve each feature sits. We then move the item left or right depending how much we intend to invest in developing the feature. Often when doing this exercise, the team will split a feature into components that might include the must-have elements and a separate set of delighter capabilities. What we want to know is how this portfolio of features we are planning for the release holds together as a whole. It is easy to fill up all your development capacity with must-have items. This is especially true if you are playing catch-up to the competition. The outcome of only including must-haves is a commodity, or "me too", product. Consider how you can sprinkle at least a little delight into the release to create differentiation that you can continue to build on in future releases. You can scope back a must-have item (*i.e.* move it a little to the left on the curve) to free up capacity for a few delighter or performance items. This is OK. There is no benefit in gold plating must-haves, because the best implementation still leaves the customer feeling neutral about them.

A few more things to consider with the Kano model:

1   Customers' expectations change over time. Thus, today's delighters, such as facial recognition on a laptop, are tomorrow's must-haves. Occasionally, you can go in the other direction, turning a must-have into a delighter. Apple achieved this in 2006 with their patented MagSafe power adaptor for their MacBook laptops. The MagSafe gave a *cool* factor to an area of the product which customers usually pay little attention to. It also added a new functional benefit that users did not expect from a power adaptor: the connector easily disconnected if someone tripped over it, protecting the laptop from getting yanked off the table and damaged.

2   Markets break down into segments. Thus, not all customers share the same values. For example, one group of laptop customers consider weight to be the top priority. This segment will gladly trade off battery life or screen size to achieve a lighter machine. For other customers, battery life is a critically important factor. You need to have a customer segment in mind when applying Kano.

3   The use of Kano as described here is as a prioritization lens. There is also a Kano survey technique that can be used to develop these curves and identify customer segments. If you pursue this route, I recommend working with a professional research firm.

4.3.5 Prioritization Matrix

The prioritization matrix is a lightweight, fast, and effective tool to help stakeholders make their beliefs explicit. Of the techniques listed in this section, it is the best method for linking the prioritization decision directly to the company strategy. Include in this process any stakeholders whose input is valuable to capture. If the team is going through this exercise for the first time, allocate two to four hours to complete it. Follow these five steps:

STEP 1: place the items the company wants to prioritize in the left-hand column. In figure 4.2, the requirements being evaluated are performance enhancements, single sign-on, integration with Salesforce.com, and support for the upcoming release of Microsoft's Internet Explorer browser.

STEP 2: develop criteria and enter them into the gray bar towards the top of the chart. In the example below, the criteria are pain for users, percentage of customers impacted, upsell revenue from existing customers, revenue from new customers, key product differentiator, and competitive necessity. Develop criteria that make sense for your context.

STEP 3: assign weights to each criterion and record them in the topmost bar. In this example, 60 percent of the weighting is for current customer criteria (pain for users, percent of customers impacted, and upsell revenue) and 40 percent is weighted to new business criteria (new customer revenue, product differentiation, and competitive necessity). The example company is ultimately indicating that it strategically values customer retention more than new customer acquisition. If, after evaluating that statement, the management team determines that new customer acquisition is more important, and that the company's current customers are not at risk, then the team would adjust the weightings appropriately. Completing this exercise is an iterative process that helps people reconcile and make explicit what they feel in their gut. The process helps all stakeholders focus on the big picture.

STEP 4: the team assigns values for each requirement. In this example, support for the upcoming release of Internet Explorer ranked highest with 60 points. The Vice President of Sales, who was representing the sales team in the creation of the matrix, might have thought Salesforce.com integration was the most important, but the matrix says otherwise. Because the Vice President of Sales helped create the matrix with the team and was part of the discussion, she understands that Internet Explorer support is a corporate priority that trumps her department's preference.

STEP 5: Sanity-check the results. If the results feel wrong to the team, it usually means the team needs to do more tuning of the weightings or values. Maybe in everyone's gut, they thought Salesforce.com integration would be the highest priority feature. Maybe the team underweighted new customer acquisition, and therefore Internet Explorer support came out on top. Once again, by having discussions around the matrix's answers, the team recalibrates its priorities and becomes aligned.

NOTE: the example here is a first-pass assessment at delivering business value. It does not take into account cost or effort. If you have good size estimates from the development team, add these as potential criteria. The criteria would need to be listed as "Low Cost" because you want a ranking of five to be the most desirable; in other words, a requirement that ranks five would be the least expensive to build. Now, since many of the requirements being ranked in this process are likely to be epics, sizing may not yet exist. In this case, take the highest-ranking requirements from the prioritization matrix, split them into features and stories, and re-evaluate once the size estimates are available.

4.3.6 WSJF Method

I first came across Weighted Shortest Job First (WSJF) in Don Reinersen's 2008 book *Principles of Product Development Flow: Second Generation Lean Product Development.* The method focuses on the cost of delay. Its later inclusion in the Scaled Agile Framework (SAFe)[38] has helped to popularize it. The method prioritizes those items that deliver the most value the soonest.

---

38   http://www.scaledagileframework.com/wsjf/

Prioritization Matrix

0 = low
5 = high

Application/Major Feature/Service	Overview	Requester	Weight[1]						Total points
			Pain for User[2] (0 - 5)	% of customers impacted[3] (0 - 5)	Upsell revenue from existing customers[4] (0 - 5)	Revenue from new customers (0 - 5)	Key product differentiator (0 - 5)	Competitive necessity (0 - 5)	TOTAL SCORE
			25	20	15	15	16	10	100
1 Performance	Reduce screen rendering to <2 second	Customers, Tech support	5	5	0	0	0	5	55
2 Single Sign-on	Allow our apps to no longer require multiple authentications	Customers	3	5	2	1	0	4	52
3 Integration with SF.com	Full data synch with SF.com database	Sales, Customers	4	2	0	2	4	0	46
4 Responsive design	Responsive design to render on mobile and tablets	Customers, Management	4	3	2	4	0	5	60
5									0
6									0

[1] Weights should total 100.
[2] Consider how difficult a feature is to use and how frequently that feature is used in assessing pain.
[3] Must take into account the % of customers impacted and their importance.
[4] You should count retaining customers who would otherwise leave as upsell revenue from new customers.

FIGURE 4.2: *Filled-out prioritization matrix*

The basic formula for WSJF is:

$$\text{WSJF} = \frac{\textbf{Cost of Delay}}{\textbf{Duration}}$$

FIGURE 4.3: *Basic WSJF formula*

It might be easier to understand through an example. In TABLE 4.2 below, in what order would you chose to develop the three features A, B, and C?

FEATURE	RELATIVE VALUE	EFFORT
A	8	4 weeks
B	8	2 weeks
C	5	4 weeks

TABLE 4.2: *In what order would you develop each features?*

If you concluded it would be best to develop the above features in the order B → A → C then you just did a WSJF calculation. WSJF for A = 8/4 = 2, B = 8/2 = 4, and C = 5/4 = 1.25. Feature B with a WSJF of four delivers the most value in the least amount of time, then feature A at two and finally feature C at one and a quarter.

WSJF can be expanded to incorporate time frame and risk components:

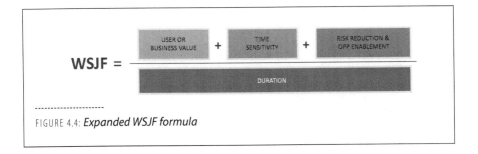

FIGURE 4.4: *Expanded WSJF formula*

Time sensitivity is a ranking on the urgency or perishability of an opportunity. The question to answer is, will the value degrade with time *or* the cost of delay increase with time? Risk reduction and opportunity enablement allow the team to better balance short- and long-term needs by investing in development that will either reduce risk later down the road — for example, if the development is based around security upgrades or scalability — or lay the foundation on which to build new capabilities, if, for example, supporting a new industry data exchange standard.

Thus, the key factors when applying WSJF are: value; time sensitivity; risk reduction and opportunity enablement; and duration/effort. The factors are scored on a relative scale using a modified Fibonacci sequence of 1, 2, 3, 5, 8, 15, 25, 40, etc. Thus, as the name suggested, WSJF measures relative value.

4.3.7 Time Sensitivity

It is always good practice to consider the lens of time sensitivity in your prioritization. Of the methods reviewed so far, only one, WSJF, explicitly incorporates this perspective. It is also important to remember that not all features, nor even all releases, are sensitive to time. But you have to consider the time dimension before ruling it out as a factor in your prioritization.[39] The four categories to evaluate are date driven, early delivery, window of opportunity, and uncertain environment (FIGURE 4.5).

---

39   Adapted from Mark Denner and Jane Cleland-Huang, *Software by the Numbers* (Prentice Hall PTR, Upper Saddle River, 2004), pp. 79 - 88.

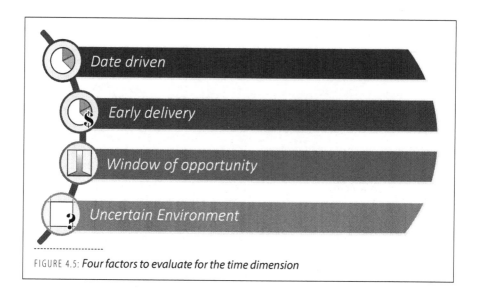

FIGURE 4.5: *Four factors to evaluate for the time dimension*

Date driven refers to releases and features that must be delivered by a given date. This usually means these projects will receive higher priority. Some businesses are seasonal. If you make tax preparation software, your product has to be out for tax season. Contractual commitments and supporting new regulations are further examples of date driven requirements. Some readers may remember Y2K (aka the year 2000 problem) — the ultimate date driven project. To save on expensive memory and storage in early computing systems, including mission critical mainframe computers, software and firmware programs stored the calendar year by the last two digits only. Thus, as the new millennium approached, these computer systems would not be able to distinguish between 2000 and 1900. Software and hardware vendors had to ensure their products would work in the new century, and they had a very real deadline by which to complete the work. Solving Y2K issues took top priority at companies across industries and nations.

Early delivery captures situations when releasing ahead of schedule would result in additional revenue. Some contracts even reward early delivery with bonuses. If you are releasing a new product, the sooner you get it in the market, the sooner you can realize revenue. In contrast, there is rarely a strong financial or market benefit for the early delivery of a maintenance release, unless it is fixing an urgent issue.

Window of opportunity refers to opportunities upon which there is only a short time to capitalize. In fast-moving technology areas, being late to market can be catastrophic. This is especially true in high fixed costs industries. In semiconductors, for example, there are short windows of opportunities where manufacturers can command a premium price for their next generation chips. If the company misses the window, it will never be able to recapture that lost revenue. Businesses that leverage fads and the news cycle have a similar challenge.

Uncertain environment describes situations where delaying a decision may improve return on investment (ROI) and product success. This situation is common in times of regulatory uncertainty or when standards are still emerging. But it can also be true if you come to a fork in your own product roadmap and need more information before deciding on which path to commit.

The United States healthcare system and providers to that system are dealing with enormous opportunity and uncertainty due to the Patient Protection and Affordable Care Act (PPACA), which was signed into law by President Barack Obama in 2010. At the heart of this legislation is universal health insurance for Americans (*i.e.* more end customers) and a shift from fee for service medicine to value-based care (*i.e.* payment for outcomes). Since its introduction, the legislation has been challenged in the U.S. Supreme Court, and Republican politicians have threatened to overturn the law.

There are no easy answers for uncertain market environments such as this. Some companies decided to take the big risk and invested heavily in establishing leadership in value-based care solutions. Venture capitalists also bet big, investing billions of dollars to fund health technology startups focused on cost-effectively improving patient outcomes. The companies and investors taking the risk believe there is a window of opportunity presented by this legislation, and that early delivery matters. Other companies have looked at the same data and have taken a more measured approach. They have concentrated the majority of their research and development budget on their traditional products, which are optimized to support fee-for-service medicine. These companies believe they can be fast followers if the Affordable Care Act is here to stay, and as health providers take on more value-based contracts. If your product was affected by the Affordable Care Act, what would you do?

4.3.8 Feature Lifecycle Method for Managing Costs and Risks

In addition to value, or, more accurately, as part of value determination, cost and risks represent two additional lenses to consider in the prioritization analysis. The ROI method explicitly includes cost, and can include a weighting for risk to create a risk-adjusted return. The WSJF method can also include risk and cost (as measured by duration). But all the other methods discussed thus far in this chapter focus on assessing value without considering cost and risk. Therefore, you need to go through a second step to include these important factors in your final determination.

4.3.8.1 Cost

In addition to understanding the benefit or value to your product of adding a new feature, you also need to determine what you are willing to pay to include that capability in your product. The cost, or relative effort, comes from your development team.[40] When evaluating cost, it is important to explain the problem to the team, rather than a preferred implementation. This creates opportunities for them to find a creative and cost-effective solution. There will, however, be times when the cost of a new capability will be more expensive or demand more effort than you anticipated. In these cases, you need to work with the Engineering team to explore alternative implementations or ways to reduce the scope of the feature to realize the primary benefit at a lower cost.

4.3.8.2 Risk

There are many types of risk that you need to manage including market, regulatory, and legal risks. You also need to consider your company's tolerance for risk, and accommodate it in your plans. Companies' varied reactions to the Affordable Care Act mentioned earlier in this chapter demonstrates how organizations have different risk thresholds.

Technical risk, similar to relative effort, is one area where you need to partner closely with your development team. First, understand how your team would like

----

40   Although beyond the scope of this book, product managers must also consider non-development costs, including sales and marketing, customer support, and ongoing support requirements in the full business case evaluation. This discussion assumes you have received approval for your product plan, and your task is to optimize the research and development investment.

to order the backlog items to i) allow the design to emerge; ii) prove or learn any new technology they intend to use; and iii) test the architecture. Next, incorporate the team's views in the overall prioritization. The idea of front-loading risk, also known as "risk first development", works well for managing technical risk as well as elements of market risk[41] (this is covered in greater detail in Chapter 6: Establishing Product-Market Fit). You improve predictability at the backend, where it is most valued. It also limits the company's investment exposure if an approach does not work out and you need to re-evaluate your plan, recast your schedule, or cancel the project.

In managing risk and costs, recognize that features, just like products, also have lifecycles. The feature lifecycle lens (FIGURE 4.6) allows you to slice a feature to identify components to accelerate and others than can safely be left until later in the project. There are four main categories to consider.

1   **PROOF OF CONCEPT** — if a feature depends on new technology or an algorithm to work, you may want to prioritize a product backlog item to demonstrate your envisioned solution will work. This is a test of basic feasibility.

2   **VALIDATED LEARNING** — this is similar to proof of concept. Use validated learning when you want early customer input into how usable a feature is or how well it solves their problem. The feature may not be generally available, but should be usable on a test system, or for selected users in the live product. Whenever you have an element of a feature for which you want user input, always ask yourself if you can test it more cost effectively by mocking it up, rather than by developing it "for real" in the product.

3   **MINIMUM MARKETABLE FEATURE** — ask yourself what is the smallest instantiation of the feature that will be usable and valuable for your users. The test for a minimum marketable feature is that users would prefer to use the feature with all its limitations rather than wait for the feature to be further enhanced.

---

41   I first learned this term and strategy from Agile expert Ron Lichty

4   **POLISH** — this is what you do to make a feature "sing" and delight users. Polishing can sometimes be an iterative process as you incrementally improve usability and support an increasing number of use cases. The feedback you get from the validated learning and minimum marketable feature implementations will help you identify the highest value areas of the feature to polish, rather than guessing at them in advance.

Not all features will require a proof of concept, but many should include validated learning and almost all should be capable of being split into minimum marketable feature and polish elements.

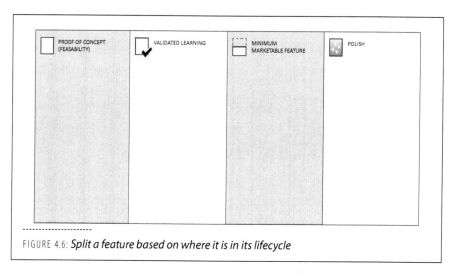

FIGURE 4.6: *Split a feature based on where it is in its lifecycle*

4.3.9 VRC Matrix

The final lens is the value, risk, cost or VRC matrix. It can help you visualize how you are allocating your investment across a "portfolio" of new features. This lens is also useful for evaluating investments across projects.

Plot each feature being considered for a release based on the value it will create and the risk or uncertainty surrounding it. Then use the size of the bubble to display cost or effort (FIGURE 4.7). In this chart, risk is an aggregation of the different risk categories including technical, market, regulatory, etc. Once all the items are plotted on the chart, evaluate how your investment is distributed amongst the four quadrants.

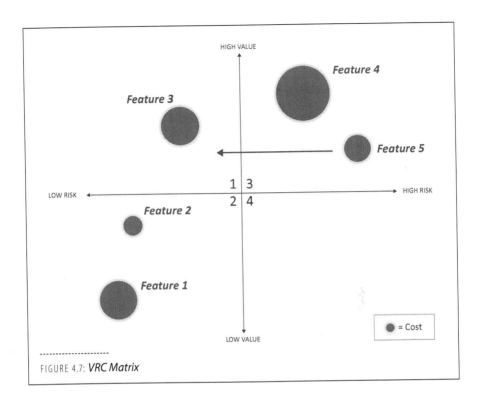

FIGURE 4.7: *VRC Matrix*

1   **HIGH VALUE, LOW RISK** — these features deliver a lot of bang for the buck. Features in this quadrant should receive high priority.

2   **LOW VALUE, LOW RISK** — inevitably, you will have many features in this quadrant. These are often driven by existing customer needs and often represent the continual improvement you need to make to your product to justify the cost of your service. In other words, many of these investments will not allow you to charge more for your product. The goal of successfully managing features in this quadrant is to try to minimize the cost, maintain customer satisfaction, and ensure that your entire development budget is not consumed by the items in this quadrant.

3   **HIGH VALUE, HIGH RISK** — features in this quadrant can often catapult your product to a new level of success. Use the feature lifecycle lens described in the previous section to see how you can slice the feature to reduce the risk and minimize cost as you prove the concept and validate it in the market. You want to minimize the investment to either move the

feature from quadrant three to quadrant one, or discontinue the feature because it does not work as planned.

4   **LOW VALUE, HIGH RISK** — ideally you should have no features in this quadrant. Take any feature in this quadrant off the backlog permanently or work to increase the value it delivers or reduce the risk.

Wrap-up

Products do not exist in a vacuum. They exist in a competitive marketplace. To develop a winning prioritization, you must understand the external factors that will influence your product's success and the objectives your product needs to achieve for itself and the company.

This chapter covered a set of frameworks and methods to assist in prioritization. Each method has its strengths and blind spots. By applying them together, you can develop a full picture of how to drive value and ensure your product stands out in the marketplace. When trying to build consensus, go through these methods with your team and stakeholders. Methods like Kano can be put on a whiteboard or printed out in large format. The team can then use sticky notes to position and split features. Always frame your prioritization in the context of your product goals and corporate strategy. Your objective with prioritization is to develop a winning plan and get your stakeholders to understand the prioritization.

NOTE: You can download many of the prioritization templates described in this chapter in the resource section at http://www.agile-excellence.com.

PART I

Summary

P art I described how the product strategy, vision, roadmap, and backlog fit together. Of the four, strategy requires the deepest thinking, and is the hardest to master. In Parts II and III, we will explore how to create a strategy that delivers growth and competitive advantage. We will look at different challenges you may face, depending on the market and your industry's lifecycle. We will examine how you can visualize your market and anticipate the future. We will also discover the central role of pricing in strategy realization and why it is a consideration that has to be dealt with upfront, during the discovery and planning stages.

This is also a good point to reflect on the stability of your strategy and plans. You can expect to re-prioritize the product backlog after every sprint as you inspect the work that was just completed and adapt to new learning that occurred during the sprint. The strategy, vision, and roadmap also get updated *as needed*, but tend to be more stable. As a rule of thumb, you will want to revisit the roadmap and product strategy at least quarterly. Often companies have quarterly planning cycles that set a regular cadence for this work. Vision should have greater longevity and stability than the roadmap and strategy but also require adjustment at times.

If you are working in an emerging or yet-to-emerge market, you will need to cycle faster than quarterly. Even in slower moving markets, there will be surprises. There are also times when you are purely exploring a concept in a research or learning mode, and you would not look to develop a full product strategy. It is the learning from this research that would eventually be incorporated into the strategy if the idea is pursued. Techniques for these situations are covered in Chapters 6: Establishing Product-Market Fit and Chapter 7: Finding Competitive Advantage.

Most of the time, especially for products in existing, recognized and highly competitive markets, the strategy is where you want to focus significant effort. Once developed, it will take less time to maintain. But it does need regular revalidation and stress testing. As new information comes in, you must ask yourself whether your strategy accommodates this information or whether the world has changed in some way that requires you to re-evaluate your plan.

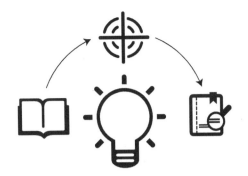

PART II

Driving
Business Success

Part II of the book covers how to develop and manage products for sustained success. This includes how to i) adjust your strategy based on the product lifecycle; ii) identify your specific product-market fit type; and iii) select the best approaches based on the level of uncertainty involved. We will be talking more about uncertainty in section 5.2, below.

Part II: Driving Business Success includes the following:

> » Chapter 5: Managing the Product Lifecycle
> » Chapter 6: Establishing Product-Market Fit
> » Chapter 7: Purposeful Learning

CHAPTER 5

- -

Managing the Product Lifecycle

P roducts and industries have lifecycles (FIGURE 5.1). Within an industry lifecycle (which can last 50 years or more) there will be many product lifecycles. You need to know where you are in both the industry and product lifecycles, and understand the specific product-market fit challenge you face. This information will help you develop your product, manage your budget, and mitigate risk. It will also influence your product strategy (Chapter 1), strategic roadmap (Chapter 3), and backlog prioritization (Chapter 4).

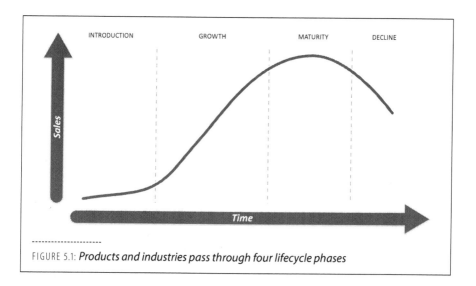

FIGURE 5.1: *Products and industries pass through four lifecycle phases*

5.1 The Product Lifecycle

Industries and products that are launched in the marketplace go through four major phases in their life: introduction, growth, maturity, and decline. Within an industry lifecycle, you will release multiple products that go through a seven-phase process from *conceive* through *retire*.[42] In the case of Software-as-a-Service (SaaS) products, the solution is never really retired and replaced with a new offering. Rather, it continually evolves to keep up with the needs of the market. Nevertheless, components of the SaaS technology may get retired, and thus present similar challenges to retired non-SaaS products, such as to how the company will migrate users from one system to the next. In all cases, the goal of each release is to retain your current customers and acquire new ones (FIGURE 5.2). Although an individual product may be in decline, your product portfolio should provide steady and growing revenue to your company.

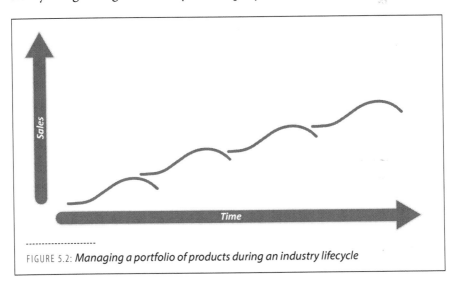

FIGURE 5.2: *Managing a portfolio of products during an industry lifecycle*

The priorities for your product, however, change throughout its and the industry lifecycle (TABLE 5.1). In the early phases of an industry, you need to educate the market. Customers need to understand what the product is and what it can do for them. Your biggest competitor at this stage is usually non-consumption. As the industry enters the growth phase, customers understand the product benefits. Your job is to make sure that the value proposition for your whole product is better for the segment of the market you serve than the value propositions of competing

---

42   The seven-phases defined by AIPMM are: conceive, plan, develop, qualify, launch, market, and retire

products. The name of the game at this phase is market share. During growth and through maturity, you need to defend your positon in the marketplace while finding opportunities to expand into adjacent areas to grow the business. Finally, to stave off decline or slow it as much as possible towards the end of the lifecycle, you need to find ways to extend the relevance of your product. During the later phases, you have to manage the cost side of the equation carefully as it becomes more difficult to earn an adequate return on investment for each dollar spent on the product.

STAGE	INDUSTRY LIFECYCLE
Introduction	All solution providers are educating the market on the problem and solution. You are competing against the status quo in this phase. Your challenge is to develop reference customers and success stories. Establish your product as the standard and safe choice, and complete your offering with services and developed ecosystem.
Growth	The growth phase tends to be a period of rapid innovation with competitors aggressively pursuing market share and new entrants competing for customers. Your challenge is to scale to meet demand. Release multiple versions of product targeted at different segments of the market. Focus on increasing differentiation.
Maturity	Market share leaders are established. Customer needs are well satisfied by products for primary use cases. Consolidation accelerates. Your challenge is to maximize profits and cash flow. Maintain full product line. Develop extensions of product to extend life of category. Consolidate position to maintain or even grow market share to gain additional scale.
Decline	The industry is contracting and continuing to consolidate. Your challenge is to harvest or divest product lines. Cut costs, reduce promotion, and shrink distribution.

TABLE 5.1: *Characteristics of each phase of the industry lifecycle*

Within each phase of the industry lifecycle, you will be releasing new and improved products and retiring your old ones. Whenever you launch a new product, you need to generate awareness for it and the new benefit it delivers. You will also want to maintain customer loyalty. You want to make it easy for your existing customers to upgrade, and give them a compelling reason to do so. During the early phases of the industry lifecycle, prioritize differentiation and revenue generation over cost cutting and margins. Controlling costs is much more critical when the market matures or is in decline.

5.2 Finding Growth

As a product manager, you need to focus your attention on growth and how you are doing relative to the market (as discussed in the Introduction). If your market is growing at 30% a year and your business is growing at 15%, you are losing share and headed for trouble. Likewise, if your market is expanding at 2.5% a year and your business is growing at 5% a year you should be proud of your accomplishment. Your strategy is working.

The Ansoff Market Growth Matrix (FIGURE 5.3) illustrates four pathways to increased revenue. In the growth phase of the industry lifecycle, you will follow a market penetration strategy. Your focus is continuing to evolve the product to better meet the needs of the market segments you serve. You may also seek to penetrate adjacent quadrants of the matrix.

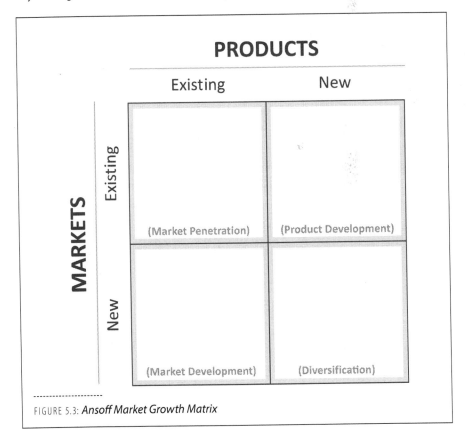

FIGURE 5.3: *Ansoff Market Growth Matrix*

As your market becomes saturated, you will have no choice but to look further afield for growth. The two safest choices are to identify new segments for your existing product (market development) or develop new products for your existing customers (product development). Market development is a scale strategy. You need to figure out how to sell what you have to more people. Product development is a depth strategy. You need to identify additional needs among your existing customers that you can meet. The product strategy work you did to understand the customer and competition is vital at this step of the process.

As the industry reaches the peak of maturity and tilts into decline, you may need to consider the riskier diversification strategy, where you enter a new market with a new product. This is known as an innovation strategy and some companies, such as Apple and Sony before them, use this method as their primary growth path. Google's parent company, Alphabet, is attempting this strategy with its moonshot projects, but the organization's success is yet to be proven. Start-ups almost always begin as innovators and then quickly move to a penetration strategy as they switch from targeting early adopters to early majority customers. Start-ups then follow with a market or product development strategy to maintain growth and improve their defensible position.

Market penetration is the easiest quadrant to navigate because this is where your business has the most knowledge and experience. At some point, however, you will need to pursue product development, market development, or diversification, and this means taking on risk and uncertainty. Businesses often struggle in managing this uncertainty, especially when diversification is needed. The tale goes something like this:

> *Once upon a time there was a startup. It launched a new product into an uncertain marketplace. With hard work and a little bit of luck the product sold. As the market grew, the business scaled to keep pace. It hired more people and devoted ever more resources to improving its products to make its customers happy. Slowly the market became predictable, and the business wanted predictability for itself too. It implemented systems and rules. It defined how decisions would be made and who would decide what. Above all else, the business wanted certainty: all products would be required to go through a consistent governing process. Thus, new products would now be held to the same*

Comcast Corporation started as a cable TV company in the late 1960s. The company has a long and storied history but the overall trajectory has been one of impressive growth, pursuing all four growth strategies (FIGURE 5.4). 1) Comcast penetrated the residential cable market well into maturity through acquisition. It also evolved its core product over the years to include premium stations, pay per view events, and the transition to digital cable to remain relevant to its customers. 2) With a physical cable connection in each customer's home, Comcast found additional products to offer existing subscribers including high speed internet and telephone, which are part of their Xfinity bundle. More recently, Comcast added home security and monitoring to their residential offering. 3) Comcast created a business division to sell its internet and phone services to a new market segment: small and medium sized businesses. 4) Comcast has also diversified, purchasing NBC Universal, which gives it video production capability, broadcast stations, and access to NBC content.

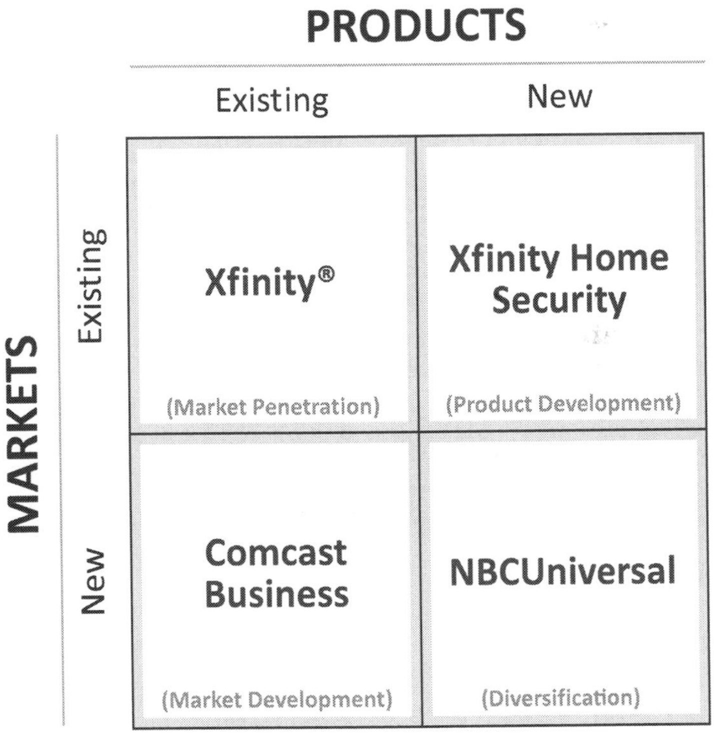

PRODUCTS

	Existing	New
MARKETS Existing	**Xfinity®** (Market Penetration)	**Xfinity Home Security** (Product Development)
New	**Comcast Business** (Market Development)	**NBCUniversal** (Diversification)

FIGURE 5.4: *Comcast Growth Strategies*

standard for reliable performance as product lines that had been in the market for many years. Thus, the business filtered out many promising opportunities where a reliable business case could not yet be developed. Over time, the business missed multiple trends, lost its ability to innovate, and could no longer drive revenue growth.

That little story describes the kind of situation many maturing businesses find themselves in. In the next two chapters we will cover some techniques to avoid the fate of the business in the story. In particular, Chapter 6: Establishing Product-Market Fit, covers how to assess uncertainty while developing a new product and the following chapter, Chapter 7: Purposeful Learning, covers how to incorporate uncertainty into your budget requests for management so your new idea is not crushed by entrenched process that exist to manage existing products.

Wrap-up

How you manage your product depends on where it is in its lifecycle, and on where your industry is in its own lifecycle. Early on, you need to focus on educating the market and growing market share. As your products mature, you need to follow-up with new and improved products to match rising customer expectations and attract increasingly cautious buyers who need to know the product is well proven. As the market matures, you need to identify new growth opportunities by expanding your footprint with existing customers, bringing your products to new customers, or entering entirely new markets.

CHAPTER 6

Establishing Product-Market Fit

A product manager's job is to achieve or optimize product-market fit. Achieving fit with the market is how product managers exert their influence and have the highest impact on the success of their companies. Doing it well requires managing three distinct areas: problem, product solution, and business model solution.[43]

PRODUCT-MARKET FIT AREA	KEY QUESTION
Problem	Is there a customer problem? Are customers willing to pay to solve it? Are there enough customers to comprise a market? Does the opportunity align with the company's mission and strategy?
Product Solution	Does the technology exist, or is your company able to be develop the technology to solve the problem? Are the technical risks manageable? Is the cost at scale below what the customer is willing to pay to solve the problem? Does your company have the design competency (in-house or through third parties) to develop the product?
Business Model	Can you cost-effectively reach your target market? Is the lifetime value of the customer significantly greater than the acquisition cost? Have you identified, and is your company able to provide or partner for, the services needed to complement the product? Can you secure the necessary funding for the project?

TABLE 6.1: *Top level questions by product-market fit area*

---

43 Historically this information was captured in the market requirements document (MRD), the product requirements document (PRD), and the business case. Many companies intermingled those documents so they lost their original purpose. For clarity, this book refers to each domain area rather than to documents types.

1   **PROBLEM** — the first step to achieving product market fit is to identify a problem worth solving. If you can answer 'yes' to the following four questions, you have identified a valuable problem worth further investigation: i) is there a customer problem? ii) Are customers willing to pay to solve it? iii) Are there enough customers to comprise a market? And iv) does the opportunity align with the company's mission and strategy? The field of design thinking has many tools for exploring and developing deep insights in the problem space.

2   **PRODUCT SOLUTION** — the next step is to evaluate whether your company can solve the problem. If you can answer 'yes' to the following four questions, the product is feasible: i) does the technology exist, or is your company able to be develop the technology to solve the problem? ii) Are the technical risks manageable? iii) Is the cost at scale below what the customer is willing to pay to solve the problem? And iv) does your company have the design competency (in-house or through third parties) to develop the product? Agile development can help you find product-solution fit rapidly.

3   **BUSINESS MODEL** — the final step is to design a sustainable business model. If you can answer 'yes' to the following four questions, the opportunity is viable: i) can you cost-effectively reach your target market? ii) Is the lifetime value of the customer significantly greater than the acquisition cost? iii) have you identified, and is your company able to provide or partner for, the services that need to complement the product? And iv) can you secure the necessary funding for the project? Market development, the basic activity of creating demand for your product, is traditionally the term used for the activity of proving out the business model. In the world of start-ups, you may also hear the term customer development.[44]

NOTE: a more complete set of questions that you must answer for each product-market fit area can be found in Appendix A.

---

44   Customer development is a theory developed by Steve Blank and described in his 2005 book *Four Steps to the Epiphany*. The book presents a systematic and iterative process for startup businesses to develop a sustainable business model.

Collectively, the three areas listed above form the product-market fit triad (FIGURE 6.1). The solution is thus made up of the product (the physical product and associated components such as update services, out-of-box experience, warranty, etc.) and the business model (how the product is priced, where it can be purchased, the level and type of service customers receive during and after the purchase decision, and third party and channel partners needed to deliver the whole solution.)

Each of the vertices of the triangle must be analyzed for uncertainty, and you must assess if a vertex's topic is known and well understood, or if significant discovery is needed. The greater the uncertainty, the more discovery required, and the more hypotheses that you will need to test. In gauging uncertainty, start by asking a binary question: is the area "defined" (well known or understood) or "undefined" (unknown or not understood)?

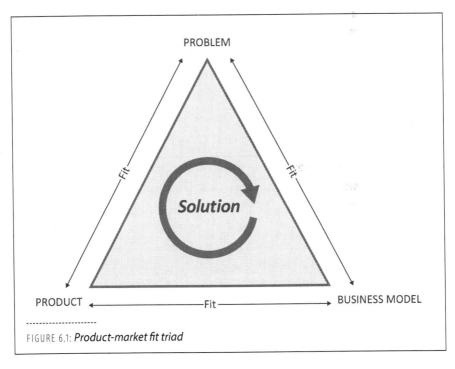

FIGURE 6.1: *Product-market fit triad*

Four distinct types of product management challenge (FIGURE 6.2) emerge from just focusing on the *problem* and *product* axes:

OPTIMIZE (TYPE I) — when optimizing, you address well-understood problems in a well-understood problem space. Optimizations often come from direct feedback from users of your products, conversations with your customers and prospects, analysis of competitive offerings, and win/loss analysis. This product management challenge is common when managing an existing product, or when entering an existing market with a "like" product. Market needs (*i.e.* the articulation of the problem) are stable. Product plans and business plans tend to be stable as well, except when the market or technology is moving faster than the development cycle. Optimizing improves the product's performance — usually along the dimensions of better, faster and cheaper.

MARKET DRIVEN (TYPE II) — this results from market research that produces fresh insights into currently unmet customer needs. It is appropriate for new products and major enhancements to existing products. Ethnographic studies and in-depth customer interviews are popular techniques for providing initial insights into possible problems a solution might address. The studies and interviews may be followed by surveys to quantify the opportunities associated with solving each problem. Market needs tend to be stable over long periods of time, but product plans and business plans can shift during the search for a good solution fit.

TECH DRIVEN (TYPE III) — tech driven is the proverbial solution looking for a problem. It comes from the insight that a technological change may provide an order of magnitude improvement in performance for a product, or enable entirely new capabilities that were previously not possible or, at least, not possible at a price the market would support. Product plans will shift until the needs for a specific target market are deeply understood. If the product enables us to solve a problem in a new way, it will share characteristics of a "visionary" product where the market needs will also shift as users learn how to apply the new technology solution to their context. Business plans can change significantly over the course of dealing with a tech driven challenge.

VISIONARY (TYPE IV) — visionary products lie so are far ahead of current customer expectations and experience that customers have trouble relating to your descriptions of the offering. Often the market for these products does not yet exist. Developing business cases around visionary products is particularly challenging, and sometimes not possible, because there exists little knowledge on which to base assumptions. Market needs, product plans, and business plans can all shift significantly. Visionary products typically create entirely new ways of doing things that were previously not possible.

As markets become more competitive and technology adoption accelerates, managing Type II, Type III, and Type IV solutions is a necessary competency for product managers.

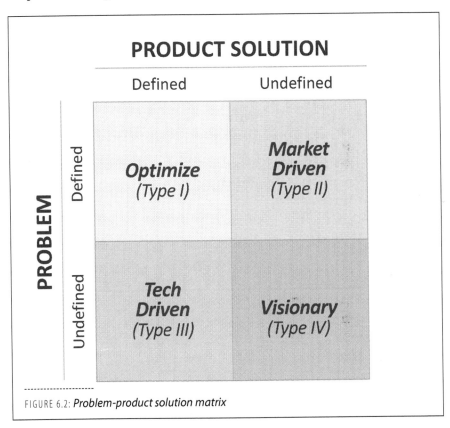

FIGURE 6.2: *Problem-product solution matrix*

Building upon the Problem-Product Solution Matrix and the four problem-product solution types, the business model will either be *defined* or *undefined*. In a defined business model, a channel already exists to reach the target market, supporting services are understood, and the pricing model is clear. In total, there are eight ways in which *Problem*, *Product*, and *Business Model* can combine, based on whether an area is defined (*i.e.* established) or undefined[45] (*i.e.* unproven) (TABLE 6.2).

45 Adaptation from D. Silverstein, P. Samuel, and N. DeCarlo, *The Innovator's Toolkit* (New Jersey: John Wiley & Sons, 2009) p. xxvi and S. G. Blank, *Four Steps to the Epiphany*, (Cafepress.com, 2006) pp. 12–16.

PROBLEM	SOLUTION	
	Product	Business Model
Optimize *(Type I)* Defined	Defined	Defined
		Undefined
Market Driven *(Type II)* Defined	Undefined	Defined
		Undefined
Tech Driven *(Type III)* Undefined	Defined	Defined
		Undefined
Visionary *(Type IV)* Undefined	Undefined	Defined
		Undefined

TABLE 6.2: *Problem, product, and business model combine to yield eight different product-market fit types. Refer to Appendix B for a full explanation with examples.*

With a variety of product-market fit challenges, you need an equally varied set of processes and measures to keep your projects on-track and minimize risk. The simplest case is when all elements (problem, solution, and business model) of the product-market fit triad are defined. The most challenging case is when all are undefined. Appendix B includes case studies that cover each of the product-market fit types and explain how the topic company successfully achieved commercial success and fit with the marketplace.

When one or more of the product-market fit triad vertices are *undefined*, project risk goes up and the ability to linearly plan and execute decreases. Iterative development and business model planning are necessary, as near-perfect gathering and analysis of upfront requirements are not possible. In an uncertain world where requirements cannot be fully understood, you cannot make upfront and accurate forecasts. Instead, you have to ask questions and generate hypotheses to be tested. In this case, you are an *explorer*.

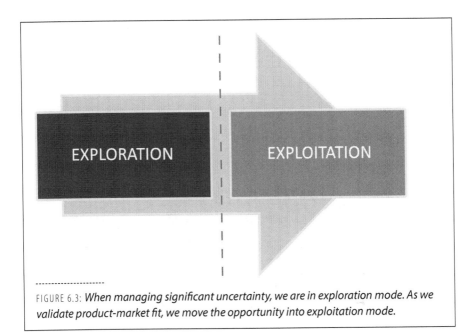

FIGURE 6.3: *When managing significant uncertainty, we are in exploration mode. As we validate product-market fit, we move the opportunity into exploitation mode.*

One the other hand, if product requirements and the business are well understood, and if you can accurately forecast and hit your targets, then you are an *exploiter*. Most business processes have been developed for exploiters with the goal of reducing variance and improving predictability. These processes support optimization and scaling.

How you approach product-market fit varies depending on whether you are an explorer or exploiter. If you are an explorer — creating an entirely new product, business model, or market — your goal is to achieve product-market fit and move the opportunity from exploration to exploitation as fast as possible. If you are an exploiter — aiming to sustain your growth or market position — you will inevitably need to allocate some investment in exploration.

6.1 Matching the Discovery and Development Processes to the Product-Market Fit Challenge[46]

Many of the companies in the case study examples in Appendix B navigated uncertain situations. The ability to adjust plans to assimilate new information was critical to their success. Agile process and Lean thinking can give you an edge in achieving product-market fit through shorter discovery and validation cycles. [47]

PRODUCT-MARKET AREA	PROBLEM	PRODUCT SOLUTION	BUSINESS MODEL
Discovery and Validation Methods	VOC Research including prototypes	Concept testing Prototypes Concierge models Purchase/Commitment A/B Testing	Conduct tests to measure customer acquisition costs, usage and retention, support costs, and project lifetime value of the customer

TABLE 6.3: *Common Discovery and Validation Methods for Product-Market Fit Areas*

6.1.1 Problem, Product, and Business Model Defined

When the problem, product and business model are all well-defined or easily definable, traditional Voice of Customer (VOC) research methods work well. The product manager should meet, talk to and observe customers who are using the company's product and the competitor's products. Usage data, when available, should be analyzed. In addition, input should be gathered from other stakeholders, such as sales, customer support and account management.

Customers and stakeholders understand the product and what it does for them. They will have strong views on what frustrates them and what could be improved. The customer will likely provide feedback by describing how they would like

----

46   This section is an updated version of the original that appeared in the eBook *Lean Product Management: Achieving Product-Market Fit in Record Time with Fewer Resources* by Greg Cohen (Silicon Valley: 280 Group Press, 2011). A free copy of this original eBook is available for download in the resource section of www.agile-excellence.com

47   Agile methods are discussed in the companion book *Agile Excellence for Product Managers* by Greg Cohen.

the product changed. You must probe to uncover the underlying problem the customer is trying to address with your or a competitor's solution.[48] You can use sketches, wireframes and prototypes to elicit additional feedback about the problem space from the customer.

Follow up with quantitative surveys to understand how many of your customers share the same problems as the interview candidates, and measure their level of satisfaction along the different dimensions of the current solution. Business cases, forecasts, and plans can be developed. The project can follow a fairly linear path of: research, prioritize, develop solution concept, validate proposed solution concept, build, launch, measure against plan and repeat.

6.1.2 Problem Undefined

If the problem is undefined or unknown, the product team needs to conduct research with the intent of discovery. As research is expensive, the team needs to prioritize which customer segments and categories of products are of interest in order to narrow the scope of the inquiry. Different techniques can be used, based on the level of uncertainty about the problem. The techniques still fall under the heading of Voice of the Customer (VOC) research. Their goal is to produce a list of problems categorized by relative importance and satisfaction with current alternatives.[49]

Out of this research comes a long list of problem statements. Quantitative analysis and surveys can then be used to score the problems uncovered in the interview and observation stages. This data is further sliced to identify segments of users who share similar viewpoints about the importance of the different problems.

In the case of the Tech Driven (Type III) challenge, the research will first focus on uncovering the general problems customers have. Further feedback can then be solicited by discussing the solution. If a working product exists, it can be given to users to actually use. For the Visionary (Type IV) challenge, the approach is

---

48   Probe means ask 'why' without sounding like a 5-year old asking "why, why, why, why, why." You can use phrases like "Tell me more", "would you describe the last time that happened", "what is the implication of that", "how do you deal with that", "what do you do next"
49   http://en.wikipedia.org/wiki/Voice_of_the_customer

similar, but you cannot expect users to be able to predict their own needs, or foresee whether the solution will solve them. The users have to be allowed to use the product and discover how it can make their lives better. Users will likely identify uses beyond even the inventors' original intent.

6.1.3 Product Solution Undefined

If the product solution is undefined, but the problem is well understood, the product team should first brainstorm potential solutions. These can then be vetted through concept testing (which includes descriptions, wireframes, and prototypes) to provide guidance about customers' interest and priorities. These are all ways to solicit user feedback in the solution space. The user is introduced to a potential solution and asked to react to it. Each concept represents a hypothesis to be tested about the priorities and trade-offs in the solution design. In general, the richer the concept test, the better the feedback.[50] Because the problem is validated, the primary question is, can an adequate solution be developed to address it? At the early stages, the product manager wants to be testing multiple concepts and the development team might be pursuing multiple solutions. Individual interviews (or a focus group) are a traditional method for gathering concept feedback. These techniques provide insight into the customers point of view (*i.e.* what they believe). Newer online methods include the use of techniques such as creating a small website or pay-per-click advertising. These tests measure interest through actual user behavior, which is a more accurate way to determine if customers truly consider the solution to be valuable. You can also A/B test different feature combinations and product positioning. The one-on-one interview is still best for deeply understanding user priorities and the basis for the priorities. Behavior tests are better at predicting what users will actually do or respond to.

For a traditional business model, where you intend to sell the product, try to close the sale as early in the process as possible. This shows that the customer perceives the solution will solve their problem and will spend money to have it do so. It also validates the price point (Chapter 11: Pricing for Competitive Advantage). If your product is ad-supported or runs on a freemium model, look for a parallel commitment from users. During research, this might be signing up to be

---

50   If you are looking for the user to help you in the design of the concept, lower-fidelity concepts may work better because the user will be more comfortable suggesting changes to them.

notified when the product is released, or for the beta program. Once the MVP[51] (Minimum Viable Product) is available, you would track usage.

6.1.4 Business Model Undefined

When the business model is undefined, it must also be tested. First, business models can be explored with qualitative models. The most promising can then be further developed in a spreadsheet to understand the key metrics and performance indicators.

Just as a product concept can be demonstrated in varying fidelities, so too can the business model. Make the solution and business model concepts appear as real as possible and seek feedback from potential users and partners. It is a good sign if the participants ask when the solution will be available. Concierge models work well for proving business models and getting to a solution fit. This is where the customer pays you for the product but i) all or large parts of the product are handled manually to confirm value can be delivered to the customer before building the product; or ii) the product is developed in close collaboration with the customer. Zappos is an example of the first concierge variant. They started by taking photos of shoes at a local store and posting them online. When someone bought a pair, they went to the shoe store, bought the pair, and shipped it off to the customer.[52] For more on the second concierge variant, refer to the Leonid Systems case study in section 6.2 of this chapter. It's worth noting that while the concierge model is good at proving the product solution fit exists and that the customer will pay, it does not prove that the business model will scale. For B2B solutions, concierge also provides the added benefit of allowing the product marketing team to have reference customers and case studies at launch, an important consideration in B2B sales.

Web-based solutions definitely have an advantage when it comes to ease of testing of the business model and its scalability. The solution can be built, and the product manager can gather data on unique visitors to the site, conversion

---

51 MVP means different things to different people. As it is used in this book, an MVP is the smallest product that will meet the need of a narrow user segment and for which the user has ideally exchanged value to use the product.

52 "Testing Your Product the Lean-Startup Way" by Lee Clifford and Julie Schlosser, Inc.com (July 17, 2012)

rates, and engagement. Other statistics that might be relevant to a given business include retention rates, core actions, number of purchases, average revenue per user, cost to acquire new users, and more. Hypotheses can be tested, and live experiments can be deployed on site to see if the changes improve the metrics and key performance indicators.

For B2B companies that sell direct, testing takes longer. New models can be tested with each sales prospect, but the time to close a deal is often measured in months — it may be up to a year — for an enterprise product. Early on, the company may create contracts with very different terms as it tests the acceptance of a new model. Whenever you have contracts with unique terms, supporting them requires additional effort from groups such as Legal, Finance, Customer Service, and Engineering. The challenge then becomes to limit the number of unique agreements as you go through the discovery phase and then convert them to standard agreements as customers reach their renewal dates. If your customer is a Fortune 500, this conversation requires finesse, and even small customers may require a delicate hand.

The hardest business models to test are those involving channel distribution. It takes time to grow channel relationships, and further time and effort to get those partners active. The product manager is competing with current revenue-generating products. Creating a productive channel takes time, and feedback is delayed. Ideally, you would work directly with customers at first. If this is not possible, work with partners to close initial sales, or bring partners in when you are about to close a sale. This way you learn from each experience until a repeatable sales process has been developed.

It should be emphasized that the direct salesforce or channel should not be scaled until the solution fit, distribution model, and pricing have been validated. The first job is selling to early customers. The next job is interviewing them to ensure the product meets their needs and discover how they are using the product. Although you should try to influence how customers perceive your products, positioning happens in the customer's mind. Therefore, you want to hear directly from the customer about what they find valuable in the solution. Ideally what they like about your offering matches what you think are its selling points, but it doesn't always happen that way. Once the positioning and sales process are validated, you can look at scaling the business.

6.1.5 Two or More Vertices Undefined

As the product-market fit triad becomes increasingly undefined, the need for quick iteration increases. Companies sometimes need to iterate to develop a simultaneous understanding of the problem, the solution, and the business model. The faster a company can iterate, therefore, the more hypotheses the company can test; the more hypotheses it can test, the more likely that the path to success will be identified. Alternatively, if a successful path does not emerge, then the faster the company can invalidate a project focus area, and the faster it can shift those resources to a more promising idea. Speed and flexibility are our friends.

Groupon started as a web platform named The Point — as in "tipping point" — to provide crowdfunding for a cause or common goal. The site drew little traffic but one set of campaigns on the site was succeeding — users organizing around saving money through group discounts. With this learning, Groupon was launched within a year singularly focused on allowing individuals to participate in group buying discounts. With problem-product fit validated well enough, it proceeded rapidly to build the service infrastructure to validate and accelerate its business model.[53]

6.1.6 Exploring Early Uncertainty in the Product-Market Fit Triad

The product-market fit canvases (*i.e.* large posters) are a specially formatted visual facilitation tool for teams to explore new opportunities through the product-market fit triad. You can download the three canvases (problem, solution, and business model) (FIGURE 6.4) from the resource section of www.agile-excellence.com. When printed, each one is three feet wide by five feet tall. Hang them on the wall in a big open room and gather the team around. The team can write directly on the canvas with magic markers, or use sticky notes. Using sticky notes makes it easier to evolve the idea. Once the team completes its exploration, take a photo to capture your work or copy it off on a worksheet. Then, clear the canvases and work through additional scenarios. The output of the effort should be:

---

53 http://www.businessinsider.com/groupon-from-the-ashes-of-a-dead-startup-to-a-billion-dollar-company-in-2-years-2011-6#in-2006-andrew-mason-founded-the-would-become-groupon-company-the-point-1

1   team alignment on the opportunity
2   identification of the largest assumptions being made and areas of highest
    uncertainty.
3   The necessary input for the development of a *learning plan*, which is
    described in Chapter 7: Purposeful Learning.

Along with the canvas downloads, there are three 8.5 inch by 11 inch worksheets
(and identical A4 versions). These can be used as an alternative to taking a photo
to capture the output of a team session or for prompting individual thinking.
Being able to see the relationship between each element can be more effective
than capturing the information in a more traditional requirements document.

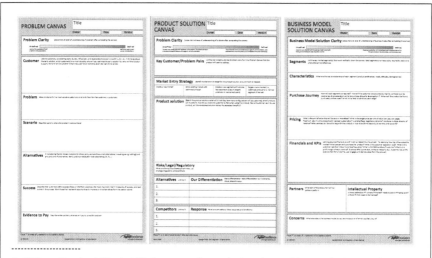

FIGURE 6.4: *Product-Market Fit Canvases for exploring the problem, solution, and business model*

6.2 Case Study — Concierge Model

My good friend Alex Cowan used the Concierge Model when he founded Leonid
Systems. Leonid Systems had a vision to make provisioning enterprise VOIP
services simpler for telecom carriers (*i.e.* a market driven, type II, challenge). A
typical process for setting up a new business customer required careful orches-
tration between three to five different network systems. It was time consuming
and difficult. The guide for doing this work might be as long as 15 pages, with lots

of opportunities to make mistakes. The team at Leonid believed they could automate the process and shrink the instructions to a one-page quick reference — or even to no reference at all.

Leonid employed a concierge model to explore the job of services provisioning. Prior to building any software, the company completed consulting engagements to streamline the process and look at the steps and parties involved. For example, how did the role of the network provisioner at the operations center relate to the job of the field technician putting phones on desks?

This consulting work helped Leonid understand both the potential value of automation as well as how to make it work in real life for the telecom company's customer. In discussions, customers expressed interest in trying a simple automation utility. Leonid's next MVP vehicle was a simple software script that accepted a flat data file and then made the correct updates to all the necessary carrier systems. The script had to be manually run by a systems engineer, which was not ideal, but this allowed Leonid and their customers to try something quick and inexpensive. Although simple, the MVP solved the primary pain point. It validated that the solution worked and a carrier would pay for the product.

Customers liked the script and expressed interest in an application that their provisioning administrators could use. The second version of the product included a frontend that provisioning admins could use to select and validate data files or manually enter information. The product was further refined and enhanced over five or six further customers. With the solution validated, the company looked to scale sales to more customers. The diversity of these new customers, particularly ones with larger IT infrastructures, created pressure to accommodate customer-specific requirements. Rather than complicate its core offering, it developed clean external interfaces, allowing custom requirements to be handled through professional services, while keeping the option open to absorb that functionality into the core product, if the functionality could be generalized.

Because Leonid sold to a narrow segment of the market, it chose to expand internationally to drive growth. Although the product was well optimized, the company faced a new, strategic challenge to its business model. It had to figure out how to cost effectively deliver quality services around the world. It settled on identifying key partners in each region that could provide consistent service and handle any specialized requirements. It then added additional features to enable partners to be successful with the solution.

Leonid worked one customer at time. It engaged the first few clients with a custom project while thinking about how to use the lessons of these projects to create a generalized product with wide appeal. In this way, the company worked iteratively towards product-market fit. With each new customer, it tested the functionality, uncovered new requirements, and validated customers' willingness to pay.

Wrap-up

The role of the product manager is to achieve product-market fit. Understanding the product-market fit challenge can help you formulate questions and corresponding tests to rapidly reduce project risk. The next chapter covers how to structure your research and sequence your work to attain product-market fit as quickly and as cost-effectively as possible.

CHAPTER 7

Purposeful Learning

As stated in the previous chapter, in many situations, creating a reliable business case, forecast, and design specification for a product is just not realistic. In describing how companies create new markets, Gary Hamel and C.K. Prahalad wrote in 1991 that "…[c]ommitment to an opportunity horizon does not rest on ROI calculations but on an almost visceral sense of the benefit that customers will ultimately derive should pioneering efforts prove successful — a deeply held belief that 'with all this benefit about, there must be a market in there somewhere.'"[54] The authors go on to further describe what they call *expeditionary marketing*, the goal of which is to understand the product features that customers value and the price and performance necessary to create a sustainable business.

Although organizations have known for a long time that business cases cannot accurately be created for all market opportunities, companies have largely ignored this reality and ceded growth markets because their process didn't allow for learning. The sooner companies, product teams, and product managers are willing to acknowledge that they don't always have all the answers, nor will they have the complete set of answers upfront, the better they will do at managing the uncertainties and risks of new product development.

---

54 "Corporate Imagination and Expeditionary Marketing" by Gary Hamel and C.K. Prahalad, HBR July — August 1991 issue

Thus, the most we can ask of any team is to deliver validated learning at all stages of the development process. To do this, you have to do two things: become a purposeful learner and create a learning plan.

7.1 Becoming a Purposeful Learner

Purposeful learners (also known as *systematic learners*) make a conscious effort to gain insights that change the way they act. They accomplish this through a structured and repeatable process that can be deployed across product teams and across the organization as a whole. Everyone on the team can be become a purposeful learner.

At a minimum, think of yourself as a learner who cycles between discovery activities and validation activities. The Discovery, Hypothesis, Test, and Learn (DHTL) (FIGURE 7.1) loop provides a little more detail on how to move between discovery and validation. It is well suited to product management and an initial problem focused inquiry. The model starts with discovery or exploratory research in an area of interest. From this first step, insights are generated for which hypotheses are developed and then tested. The resultant learning sets up the next DHTL cycle. You want to quickly match-up a problem with an intended product and business model solution. First you create an insight through discovery and then you see if you can validate a fit with a potential solution. The discovery loops usually start as qualitative research to identify customer problems that are underserved by current solutions. As you progress, discovery becomes more quantitative to identify market segments that share the same unmet need, and solution-focused to identify whether your envisioned solution will meet the need.

In addition to DHTL, there are other learning cycles that can be applied to reach validation and may be better suited to your context:

1 **PDCA** — Plan, Do, Check, Act is also known as the Deming cycle.[55] This model assumes the scientific method can be applied, and that a statistically significant data set can be acquired. It works very well for web analytics and quantitative studies.

---

55   Also known as PDMA for Plan, Do, Measure, Act or PDSA for Plan, Do, Study, Act

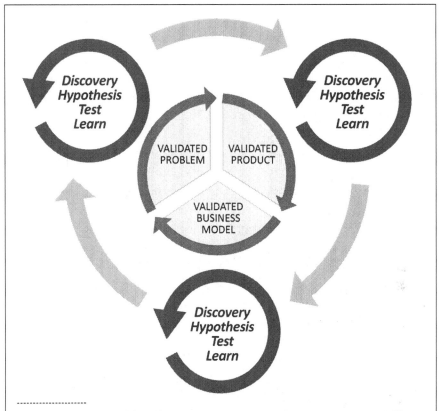

FIGURE 7.1: *Producing validated learning requires many cycles to converge on a viable product-market fit. It also requires some resets when a hypothesis turns out to be false.*

2 **INSPECT AND ADAPT** — make frequent inspections to ensure the project is moving in the right direction and adjust the plan based on the new information. Inspect and adapt is perfect for empirical processes usually associated with creative endeavors where new knowledge is learned from experience. The Scrum framework is based on this model.

3 **OODA LOOP** — Observe, Orient, Decide, Act was developed by Air Force colonel John Boyd as a decision making framework for fighter pilots to approach a combat situation, out-tempo their adversary, and disrupt their opponents' decision cycle. The US Marine Corps incorporated many of Boyd's ideas in their doctrine of maneuver warfare. When applied to business, it works well for product strategy: *observe* is the data collection

and five inputs (figure 1.1 from Chapter 1: Product Strategy), *orient* is the situational awareness of customer and competitors that comes from your observations and analysis, *decide* is your recommendation and hypotheses to be tested, and *act* is the execution of the strategy. OODA explicitly incorporates cultural context, an essential consideration in product strategy, that takes into account customer expectation and anticipated competitive response. With the continuous application of the OODA loop, you can navigate an ever changing landscape.

4   **BUILD, MEASURE, LEARN** — this model, promoted by Lean Startup, seeks to design the simplest product test possible, validate it with customers, and feed the learning into the next round of tests.[56] This is the reverse of the typical phase-gate process, in which the team tries to research and analyze everything upfront before starting to develop the solution. The key strength and limitation of build, measure, learn is its "solution first" focus.

Within all these processes, the core is to describe how you believe the world works and test it frequently. I also refer to this as *Always Be Validating* (ABV). To make it work you should never go too long without validating with the customer.

7.2 Creating a Learning Plan

Learning plans offer many of the same benefits as a business plan but, instead of an ROI, they promise to deliver the knowledge necessary to make a better-informed decision on the allocation and commitment of resources. A learning plan lays out the learning objectives, the cost of gathering that learning, and the decision points where your executive sponsors can re-evaluate the project to control risk.

To create a learning plan, use the product-market fit triad canvases (or the expanded list of question in appendix A) to generate key questions or assumptions behind your opportunity. Then prioritize the list by criticality (*i.e.* riskiest assumptions). It has been my experience that at any point while researching an opportunity,

---

56   http://theleanstartup.com/

there are one or two critical questions that have to be answered. If they cannot be resolved, then subsequent questions are irrelevant. For example, I worked on one product where the team needed to know if we could secure a patent to protect the intellectual property (IP) rights. If the research came back negative, all the other questions (such as whether consumers would be interested in the product, could it be manufactured at a low enough price point, could we secure distribution) would not matter. Our patent search turned up prior art. We would not be able to protect the idea to the level we needed and decided not to pursue it further. We did not need to build anything. There was no need to size the market, develop a business case, or even do customer research. The lesson is to start with the one or two questions that really matter to the success of your product.

Once you have the prioritized list of questions, estimate your confidence that you know the answer. Then ask i) how you might test your hypothesis around the question; ii) how confident you will be after the test; and iii) the time and funding you need to complete the test (FIGURE 7.2). For each question, try to identify two or three tests. This will give you flexibility when it comes to assembling the *key question chain*™ that is the backbone of the learning plan. This is done in the next step.

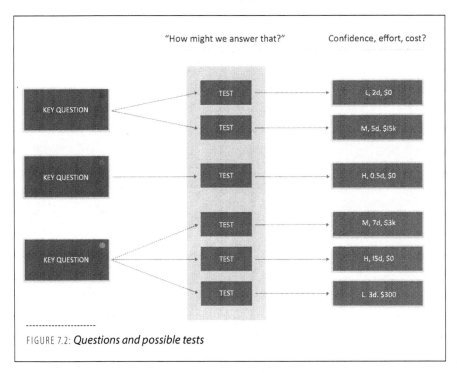

FIGURE 7.2: *Questions and possible tests*

Once the question-test pairs have been created, link them together to generate an optimized learning plan (FIGURE 7.3). This is called the *key question chain.*

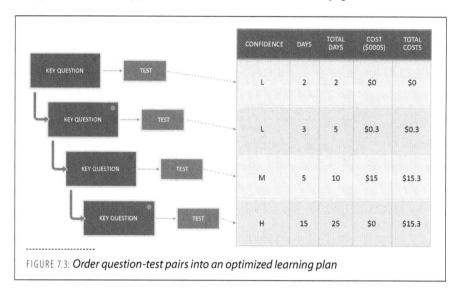

FIGURE 7.3: *Order question-test pairs into an optimized learning plan*

Let's look at an example that incorporated multiple tests and was ultimately a long question chain. During the dotcom boom, I was working on a visionary (Type IV) product-market fit challenge. It was a multi-stakeholder business model. The application would be branded to a major retailer, such as Blockbuster Video (who we'll look at again in Part III), and consumers would earn loyalty points towards products from that retailer that were subsidized by a cost-per-click advertising network.[57] We had a lot to validate, from "can we even sign a retail partner?" to "will consumers download and stay engaged with the product?" We set about creating a learning plan, and, because this was a visionary (Type IV) challenge, the team felt we had to run the test in the "wild". We took 90 days to create a working prototype and another two months to complete a true working system that could be deployed. This was fast for that point in history.

Once the prototype was complete, we started showing it to retail partners. This was the first and ultimate test — would a client sign an agreement for our product

57   At this point in history, the world of online advertising was in the early phases of the lifecycle and much of what we take for granted today did not exist. Cost per click (CPC) advertising was new, and starting to unseat cost per impression (CPM) ads. We also needed a direct sales person on staff to sell our limited advertising inventory, because syndicated advertising networks were not available.

A number of years back, I was working on a consumer product for the home. It fell in the market driven quadrant (Type II) of the product-market fit types. The product was going to be expensive to manufacture. One of the early questions, after we had confirmed the product was of interest to consumers, was whether it could command a high enough price point to be profitable. We identified three ways to test this (table 7.1) and ultimately used the first two.

FEATURE	CONFIDENCE	DAYS OF EFFORT	COST	DURATION (DAYS)
Look at market for similar products	L	1	$0	1
Create a concept document and conduct a survey	M	2	$0	20
Create a microsite, market it, and take pre-orders	H	5	$5K	45 - 60

TABLE 7.1: *Three tests to answer price point question*

Looking at the market for similar products was a quick and easy test. We invested in this test before the others for that very reason. Although it gave us some directional comfort, we were not confident in moving forward with product design and manufacturing analysis, because the product idea did not have strong parallels in the home market. Next, we created a concept document with an accompanying pricing survey. This allowed the team to bound the low and high price points for the product and get a sense of elasticity. We felt confident enough in the results of the survey to move forward with the product design and deeper cost analysis (you can read more about this story in Chapter 11: Pricing for Competitive Advantage).∎

and service? We passed! In a few months we had commitments from a handful of retail partners willing to deploy the product.

The second question we had to answer was whether consumers would adopt the product. We also had a secondary issue that needed to be addressed: we needed to know how consumers might try to "game" the system to earn undeserved loyalty rewards. To retain our retail partners' trust, we needed to ensure that no fraud occurred on the system from day one. We once again concluded that the only way to test this was in the wild.

Should you build your learning plans with open ended questions or hypotheses? The answer is both. Learning plans have a question and a test. The team should first formulate a question and then generate a hypothesis or prediction for each test.

If you chose to conduct a survey, team members should take a moment to predict what they expect the survey results will be. By having a hypothesis, the team will explicitly confront data that does not support the anticipated outcome. If the team does not generate a hypothesis, they will justify any result with a convenient explanation and miss an opportunity to learn.■

We created a rewards site that we controlled where users earned points towards free movie tickets from a major cinema brand, and other prizes. We underwrote and fulfilled all the rewards ourselves, which was well worth the costs and effort for the knowledge we were gaining. We then seeded the site on a known online community that discussed less than ethical ways of taking advantage of companies. We had the users that we wanted for our beta test. We could track their actions, and, for the less well-intentioned segment, we could also read their online community discussions. Over the next couple of months, we released regular updates to the code to eliminate vulnerabilities exposed by the users. We also identified and started tracking metrics to recognize patterns of fraud. By the end of the beta period, we had a robust system to take to market.

To summarize this example, the first question we had to answer was related to the business model. Could we sell the idea to a retail partner? Second, we had to test the desirability of the solution with consumers. Third, we had to know we could ensure the integrity of the system. These were the three key validations that needed to occur, and, in our case, we felt the only way to truly know was to do it for real — sell the system and run a beta with real users on the real product. Although more expensive and time consuming to implement, these were all tests that would provide high confidence in the learning outcomes.

7.3 How Fast Can You Learn?

With the rapid pace of change, we must lead our teams to out-learn, out-develop, and out-innovate the competition. So how fast can an organization really move? In the examples in the learning plan above, key lessons were realized on time frames of days to months. Let's look at two examples of companies pushing the upper limit of what's possible. Moving at this speed is ambitious and takes full commitment from a cross-functional team. I hope it inspires you to challenge your own beliefs about how fast you can learn.

7.3.1 Nordstrom Labs

Nordstrom staff observed that customers, when shopping for sunglasses, would often take pictures of themselves with their smartphones. Nordstrom Labs asked the question of whether they could develop a product to support the shopping experience (*i.e.* a market driven, type II, challenge). The team did a five day "flash build".[58] They set-up their workspace right in the sunglass department of Nordstrom's flagship store in Seattle. On day one, they observed and spoke with customers buying sunglasses, created a user story map,[59] and developed paper prototypes that they used to elicit feedback. By day 2 they had a working iPad prototype where the user could snap a photo wearing one pair of sunglasses, repeat the step with a second pair and then compare the photos side-by-side. The team continued to gather feedback on each feature as they developed it to improve the design. They added a field so the photos could be named with sunglass brand or model, since customers may try on a lot of different styles, switched to a fixed orientation in landscape to avoid issues with viewing the screen with polarized sunglasses, and allowed the user to flip the camera view so the salesperson could take a picture when assisting a customer, or the customer could take their own photo if using the application by themselves. By the end of day five, the team had a functional application with a fair amount of polish that simplified the experience of shopping for sunglasses.

---

58 https://youtu.be/szr0ezLyQHY
59 User Story Mapping is a visual technique developed by Jeff Patton to focus a team on the user's journey through the product

What happened next is equally interesting. The team left the application at the store and came back a few months later to collect more feedback. During that time, sales reps had stopped using the application and had reverted to using the standard iPad camera. The reps did not understand what made the Nordstrom's application useful and different. The team spent additional time to further improve the application for the sales people and, most importantly, train them on the benefits of the solution. The big lesson here is that the Innovation Lab achieved problem-product fit but failed at product-business model fit. Training, which is part of the whole product, was a necessary component for adoption.

7.3.2 Rekindle

When Mike Lisavich co-founded Rekindle in December 2013, he faced a technology driven (type III) challenge with business model undefined. Rekindle had a nascent referral technology that could take data from contact lists such as phone and email, build out a social map, identify strength of connection, and recommend the best mutual "friend" for a referral to go through. The timing seemed right to take this technology to market, in that both Facebook and LinkedIn were restricting access to their developer APIs. Rekindle would not need to compete against solutions leveraging either of those giant social networks.

The company adopted Design Sprints, a method developed by Google Ventures (one of the company's investors), where teams work through an intense five-day design thinking cycle:

1　MONDAY — set the goals, questions to be answered, and investigate the problem
2　TUESDAY — ideate and refine possible solutions
3　WEDNESDAY — vote on the most promising solutions, storyboard them, and further develop the concepts
4　THURSDAY — create a realistic enough prototype to test it with real users
5　FRIDAY — interview customers, test the prototype, and synthesize the learning.

Design sprints ensure the team is frequently testing with customers. In the early sprints, the team would test three to four prototypes on Friday. Mike found that testing at this speed was much more capital efficient than taking an extra week to perfect any given concept. By the time development was ready to work on the product, 90% of the front-end was validated.

Of course, prototype testing only gets you so far. Nothing beats observing real user behavior and thus the need for getting an MVP into the market sooner rather than later. Rekindle launched their first product in the personal dating segment in August 2014. The core sign-up and basic outcome flows were already well vetted from the design sprints. Early retention was great, but at the 30-day mark engagement was dropping off. Users were uncomfortable asking their friends for multiple introductions.

In November 2014, the company pivoted to B2B. They employed design sprints again to explore a solution targeted at sales professionals. Five sprints alone were devoted to the difficult challenge of ranking and presenting the referrers based on the strength of their connection to the contact. Unlike the consumer market, sales professionals were completely comfortable asking for multiple introductions. Mike and his team realized that they had built the right feature all along but had initially targeted the wrong problem or use case to solve. With version two, they had a winner.

Hubspot, a leading inbound marketing and sales platform, immediately saw the potential of Rekindle's technology. The company acquired Rekindle for use in their Sidekick product. Sales representatives would now be able to request warm introductions through other team members.

In just under 18 months, Rekindle went from an idea to an acquisition. During this time, they conducted over 15 design sprints, interviewed over 50 prospective users, and explored both B2C and B2B market segments. Most importantly, they validated their technology and were able to sell it for ultimate commercialization.

7.4 Piecing It All Together

Applying the concepts discussed in this chapter to a project looks like this:

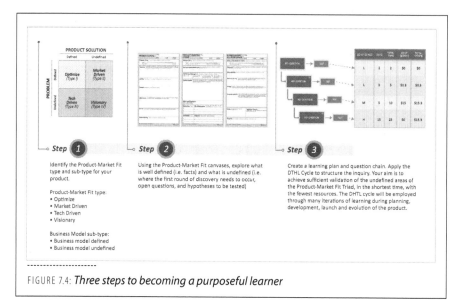

FIGURE 7.4: *Three steps to becoming a purposeful learner*

Wrap-up

Sometimes you're an explorer and sometimes an exploiter. Sometimes you can test with a concept document, sometimes a prototype works better, and other times only the actual product will do. Likewise, sometimes you can create a reliable business plan, and sometimes you need a learning plan.

At some point in the process, you must try to sell the product, and the sooner the better. If you can produce a scoped-down version of the product, or produce it in small quantities and sell it, great! If you can take preorders, great! For enterprise software, even getting a five-figure commitment for concept development is a good proof point. Testing the customers' willingness to exchange value is a necessary validation. Everything else is just talk.

Lastly, for teams to successfully work in tight loops of discovery and validation, the development processes has to match. Agile development methods support rapid learning loops. Optimize (Type I) is the only product-market fit type where traditional serial development may still be considered, and may be preferred for legacy code bases where the cost of change is high because of code interdependencies and lengthy testing procedures.

PART II

Summary

As you search for sustained growth, your number of products, or versions of your offering, will expand. Your business will need to select a core strategy: will you look to service more of the needs of your existing market, take the current product to new markets, or create entirely new products for new markets? As you pursue new products, new markets, new technologies, and new business models, you will face varied challenges in achieving product-market fit. You will need to adjust your plan to the circumstance and master purposeful learning.

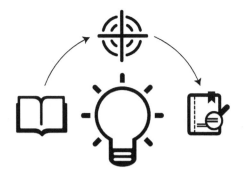

PART III

Finding Competitive Advantage

This section of the book covers how to achieve competitive advantage over the long-term. As the speed of business accelerates, small differences in your strategy and the execution of your strategy magnify. Through superior analysis, you can gain a sustainable advantage over your competitors and continually calibrate your approach to an ever-evolving market.

The *Finding Competitive Advantage* section includes the following:

» Chapter 8: Basic Strategies and SWOT Analysis
» Chapter 9: Anticipating the Future with Industry Analysis
» Chapter 10: Mapping Your Markets
» Chapter 11: Pricing for Competitive Advantage

As you read these chapters, you will be introduced to a set of complex models and big concepts. If you earned an MBA, this will be a refresher, an update, an introduction to some new material, and a reminder to put these ideas to use. If this is the first time you are being exposed to these concepts, it is a lot to absorb. Consider consulting the referenced source material for further reading. Regardless of your existing level of knowledge, as you work through this section, keep in mind the end goal: identifying where your organization can better serve a market segment and gain a sustainable advantage over the competition.

CHAPTER 8

Basic Strategies and SWOT Analysis

B asic strategy frameworks capture how companies compete. They highlight logical patterns that are common across industries and periods of corporate history. You can use them to categorize your company and competitors. They tend to illuminate how a company views opportunities in the market, and provide a good starting point for understanding how a company will continue to compete.

Although basic strategy frameworks are useful, do not let them limit your thinking. Companies will not fit perfectly into the frameworks, and neither should your strategy. Michel Porter, in his book devoted to generic strategies, specifically states that "the best strategy for a given firm is ultimately a unique construction reflecting its particular circumstances".[60] Nevertheless, basic strategies provide a starting point on which to layer analysis that will help you uncover marketspace that you can own.

---

60   Competitive Strategy: Techniques for Analyzing Industries and Competitors" by Michael E. Porter (The Free Press, New York, 1980), p. 34.

As you read this section on basic strategy, you may note similarities with strategy frameworks from Michael Porter and *The Discipline of Market Leaders* by Michael Treacy and Fred Wiersema. Decades after their works were published, I still find the frameworks useful and consider them when performing competitive analysis. I find, however, that they do not always fit into the way I like to visualize the market landscape. I also find it helps to separate where to compete from how to compete (I credit Cliff Bowman of Stratevolve for this insight.)[61] As a product manager, separating where and how appeals to me in the same way I find it valuable to separate the problem and solution space when analyzing product-market fit. You should decide for yourself the framework that best captures your industry.

61   For further reading on the limitations of some of the most well-known basic strategy frameworks refer to "Generic Strategies: a substitute for thinking?" by Cliff Bowman of Stratevolve.

8.1 Basic Strategy — Where to Compete

Where to compete covers the product area and market segments in which a company participates. *Where* can be divided into three basic strategy types: scale, depth, and innovation. Let's look at each one in more detail.

Scale

Companies that pursue scale replicate their solution in as many markets as possible. They are positioned *horizontally* with a product offering that cuts across markets. This strategy enables the company to realize cost efficiencies in research and development, or in operations. Platform companies typically follow this approach. Oracle released the first commercial SQL relational database management system in 1979. In 1983, it had rewritten its application in the C programming language to allow for easy porting across operating systems and markets (*e.g.* business, government, research). In this early phase of the company's history, it was dependent on other vendors to provide useful applications to run on top of the Oracle database. Later in its history, it began developing application suites (a depth strategy). Cognex is another scale company. It produces machine vision systems for automated manufacturing. It initially focused on semiconductor and electronics assembly, and then applied its technology to manufacturing applications in industries as varied as automotive, food and beverage, logistics, packaging, and pharmaceuticals.

Depth

Companies that pursue a depth strategy create multiple products to meet different needs within a vertical market. These companies understand the market's needs within their vertical well. They create solutions, often fully integrated and with supporting services, to assist their customers in achieving their broader business goals. Because companies that use a depth strategy are focused on a vertical, they have a smaller market (compared to scale players) on which to spread their R&D investment for any given product. They do, however, gain efficiencies in sales and marketing by being able to sell multiple products to the same customer. Cerner Corporation develops information technology solutions for the healthcare industry. The company has a broad product line with solutions to manage physician practices, electronic health records, pharmacies, population health, point of care, billing, and more. KLA-Tencor is another depth company. It produces process control and yield management equipment for the semiconductor industry. The merger of KLA and Tencor in 1997 brought together defect inspection with metrology. The company has continued to expand its portfolio of technologies and products to meet the needs of semiconductor manufacturing clients.

Innovation

Innovators pursue novel solutions that can be in diverse product and market segments. Start-ups by their very nature usually start as innovators solving a narrow problem in a single market. They serve their target market until the company gains a beachhead and can then pursue growth by going deep or going for scale. Some mature companies, however, make innovation their primary strategy. Apple, for example, with its MacBook Air, iPod, iPhone, and iPad, upset or created markets for ultra-laptops, MP3 players, smartphones, and tablets respectively. Amazon innovates across a large range of products and markets including e-commerce, consumer electronics such as Kindle e-readers, Fire tablets, Fire TV, and the Echo speaker; plus digital media streaming, platform technologies such as Alexa voice services, and their cloud computing offering, Amazon Web Services.

If we refer to Ansoff's Growth Matrix (covered in Chapter 5: Managing the Product Lifecycle), a framework for working out where to compete, we can see that scale maps to market penetration, depth maps to product development, and innovation can map to any of the four quadrants. Further, as companies grow, they often employ two of the strategy types concurrently, such as depth in one market vertical and scale across a single product area.

One of the most unlikely match-ups in history was Pampers vs. the Huggies/ Kimbies brand disposable diapers. The first Pampers disposable launched in 1961, and Huggies appeared in 1976. The worldwide market for disposable diapers was growing explosively. Proctor and Gamble (P&G), the maker of Pampers, is a depth company focused on meeting the diverse needs of the homemaker. Kimberly-Clark, the maker of Huggies and Kimbies, is a scale company with roots in the paper pulp business. P&G saw a need they could fulfill for mothers and Kimberly-Clark saw a growth market for cellulose, the primary material in the absorber. For two companies with dominant brands in the personal care market, there is less competitive overlap between their product lines than one might expect until you know the context of their strategies. Although P&G entered the paper products market with Charmin in 1957, the company is unlikely ever to expand into the disposable apparel market for industrial and professional markets that Kimberly-Clark services. On the other hand, although Kimberly-Clark sells cleaning wipes, it is just as unlikely to enter the market for laundry detergent on which P&G focuses.[62]

---

62   The history of the disposable diaper can be found at http://disposablediaper.net/general-information/disposable-diaper-history/. Additional historical information for this section came from http://www.kimberly-clark.com and http://us.pg.com/

8.2 Basic Strategy — How to Compete

In addition to deciding *where* to compete. A company must also decide *how* to compete. For this, there are three positions: *leadership, value,* and *low cost. Leadership* companies focus on delivering superior capability or performance at a premium price. *Value* companies focus on delivering a high value to price ratio, and *low-cost* companies look to compete almost purely on price (FIGURE 8.1).

Amazon is a value brand. Its products pack a lot of capability along with unique Amazon ecosystem features. Their position was highlighted in Chapter 2: Vision in the discussion of how Amazon priced its Kindle Fire tablet at less than half the cost of the Apple iPad. To repeat Jeff Bezos' quote from that chapter, in which he alluded to Apple:

"There are two types of companies: those that work hard to charge customers more, and those that work hard to charge customers less. Both approaches can work. We are firmly in the second camp."

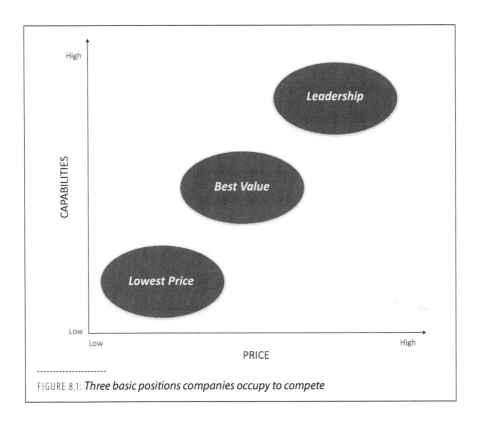

FIGURE 8.1: *Three basic positions companies occupy to compete*

There are lower priced tablets in the market than the Kindle Fire. These are produced by low-cost strategy companies. Amazon works to maximize value to price and looks to find a middle ground where it can deliver a lot of capability at an affordable price. Apple, on the other hand, is an innovator that enters markets where it can establish product leadership and command a premium price for it.

These positions work because customers are not homogenous. Customers cluster into segments that place different levels of significance on capabilities, price, and qualitative criteria such as brand. Likewise, a company may compete in multiple segments, often with different branding, and primary segments can often be divided into sub-segments. Uber is an interesting case: a company that operates under the single parent name and competes effectively in all three value categories. UberBlack Lux and SUV serve the premium end of the market; UberX, XL and Select are higher-value alternatives to taxis; and UberPool trades convenience for lower cost as riders going to different destinations carpool by sharing a single Uber.

Capabilities also encompass the different dimensions of the whole product, such as support, training, warranty, financing, and pricing. The e-commerce company Jet.com offers a lower price on products if the customer opts out of free returns or pays by debit card. Both of these options allow the consumer to save money by accepting a lower level of service and convenience. I worked for a client that maintained US-based technical support as a way to increase capability for a product at the high-end of the value position.

8.3 Niching

Niching is when a company selects to serve a narrow segment of the market with a product that matches that segment's unique needs and preferences. Companies choose niching when they will struggle to succeed in the mainstream market.

In the highly competitive laptop market, Panasonic carved out a niche for ruggedized laptops with their Toughbook® line of computers. They followed that with the Toughpad® line of hardened Android tablets that are designed to endure heat, cold, water, dust, and being dropped. Panasonic's Tough line is sold across multiple vertical markets, and the products command a price premium for the added performance. Alienware, on the other hand, has manufactured high-performance laptops, desktops, and servers for serious gamers since 1996.[63] Alienware focuses on a narrow market. Hightail (formerly YouSendIt) is another company that selected a niching strategy when faced with intense competitive pressure after nearly a decade of success. Its story is covered in Appendix B: Business Model Undefined.

The challenge for companies that choose niching is growth. They may dominate a segment, and that might be the best choice given the business's position in the marketplace. Nevertheless, it can be hard to cross over to the mainstream market if growth levels out, and they remain more vulnerable to changes in their own markets.

---

63   Alienware was purchased by Dell in 2006 and operates as a subsidiary, retaining control of its design, marketing, and brand name.

8.4 SWOT

SWOT is an acronym that stands for *strengths, weaknesses, opportunities* and *threats* and is a classic analysis framework for evaluating your company and competitors (FIGURE 8.2). Strengths and weaknesses are internal factors about the company being analyzed. These can include core competencies, intellectual property, market position, and access to capital to list a few. Opportunities and threats refer to the external environment. These can include shifts in technologies, markets, regulations, and so on.

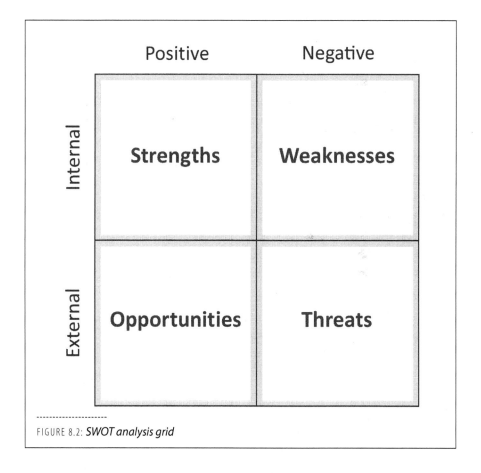

FIGURE 8.2: *SWOT analysis grid*

Once the grid is filled out, you should determine action items to take advantage or mitigate risks that the SWOT analysis has surfaced. Even doing this, I have found there are a few challenges with getting the most out of a SWOT. The first is that comparing SWOTs for different companies is difficult because a SWOT is just a group of four lists. Further, SWOT does not capture a good picture of a competitor's current strategy. Therefore, how each item in the SWOT relates to a company's present plan is not apparent. Lastly, the entries are not weighted. For example, a SWOT may contain six items under opportunities, but it will be hard to infer which ones are more likely to be pursued.

What is missing from SWOT is a way to visualize strategy and the differences between companies. SWOT, in particular, lacks a way to provide context for the analysis. To solve this, I turn to Market Maps; a technique described chapter 10.

Wrap-up

By understanding basic strategies, we have a starting point for analyzing our own company and competitors. It is important to evaluate both *where* to compete and *how* to compete. SWOT provides an additional framework to assess a company's strategic situation and options, but is most effective combined with a Porter's Five Forces (Chapter 9) and Market Map (Chapter 10) Analyses.

CHAPTER 9

Anticipating
the Future with
Industry Analysis

A s mentioned in Chapter 5: Managing the Product Lifecycle, industries follow lifecycles. As an industry matures, the market and competitive landscape evolve. Understanding an industry's structure and how it is changing is essential to developing and evolving your product strategy.

9.1 Five Forces Analysis

Porter's Five Forces[64] provides a framework for assessing an industry's current state and how it will evolve. The model was developed by Harvard Professor Michael E. Porter in the late 1970s. It identifies five industry forces (FIGURE 9.1) that determine the competitive intensity and attractiveness of an industry.

----

64   The discussion of Porter's Five Forces in this section is largely drawn from a 2008 article updating the original model. "The Five Competitive Forces that Shape Strategy" by Michael Porter, Harvard Business Review (January 2008).

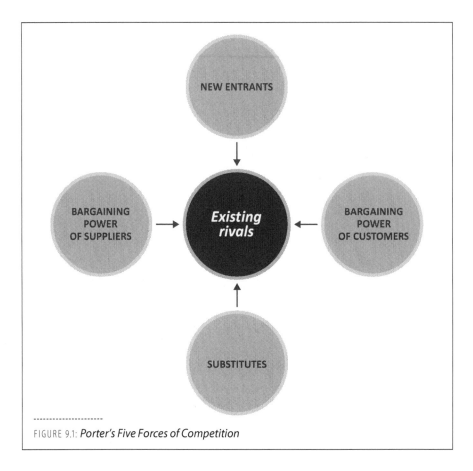

FIGURE 9.1: *Porter's Five Forces of Competition*

The five forces are threat of rivals, threat of new entrants, threat of substitutes, bargaining power of suppliers, and bargaining power of customers.

1   THREAT OF RIVALS

Rivalry between competitors is where companies traditionally focus their attention. It is the most immediate threat. Rivalry increases when many companies compete with similar strategies. It intensifies when market growth flattens and businesses can only grow by luring customers away from each other. When companies resort to price competition, industry profits transfer to customers as cost savings, and industry profitability declines.

2   THREAT OF NEW ENTRANTS

Many of the traditional barriers facing new entrants to many industries — scale, brand equity, and capital requirements, among others — have diminished in recent years. As such, the threat to existing businesses is particularly acute. To give just one example, Software-as-a-Service business models hosted in the cloud on reliable, scalable infrastructure using open source software have reduced the investment and scale required to launch a software business by orders of magnitude.

In their 2009 article "The Consumer Decision Journey", McKinsey described how search (e.g., Google, Bing) has shrunk the advantage of brand equity.[65] Before internet search, when a need emerged, consumers would only consider brands of which they were already aware. But with search, new entrants, even brands that consumers had never heard of, enter the decision cycle. Effective search engine optimization and online advertising campaigns can help new entrants be considered at the critical point in the decision cycle even when prior brand awareness does not exist.

One the other hand, network businesses,[66] for example Facebook, create a significant barrier to new entrants and can quickly achieve global scale. The failure of Google+ (Google Plus), which launched in 2011, to directly rival Facebook offers a powerful example of how a well-resourced entrant could not overcome the network effect advantages that protect an established player. Only companies with significantly differentiated products and value propositions, such as Snapchat and Pinterest, have been able to compete side-by-side with Facebook, although on a smaller scale.

When the threat of new entrants is high, profit potential becomes limited. This situation is particularly acute when new entrants are moving from adjacent market spaces and can use existing cash flow to fund their market share growth in the new market. If the threat of new entrants is high, incumbent companies can protect their market position by keeping prices down and increasing investment to improve their products and services.

---

65   http://www.mckinsey.com/business-functions/marketing-and-sales/our-insights/
the-consumer-decision-journey
66   Porter refers to this as a "demand-side benefit of scale"

3   THREAT OF SUBSTITUTES

Substitutes have long presented a threat to businesses. Uber and other ride-sharing services are posing a significant danger to the age-old taxi business. Likewise, similar but less capable products can be substitutes as well. Smartphones replace the need for basic digital cameras and camcorders. Video subscription services such as Netflix offer a substitute for network TV, and YouTube is a substitute for both.

Non-consumption, or doing without, is also a substitute. Scott Cook, the founder of Intuit, was famous for saying the biggest competitor to their Quicken financial software was the pencil. Because of this insight, Cook did not focus on out-featuring other personal finance competitors, but rather on making Quicken easier to use than a paper checkbook.

4   BARGAINING POWER OF SUPPLIERS

When power is concentrated in the hands of suppliers, costs may be shifted to other industry participants. Further, if your industry has intense rivalry, you may not be able to pass on supplier price increases to your own customers. This situation results in lower profitability for the industry. It is particularly acute if your industry is only one of many that the supplier supports.

Suppliers also have power if they offer highly differentiated offering or where there are no substitutes. Suppliers have power when switching costs are high. Suppliers may also pose a threat as a new entrant if they chose to forward integrate (*i.e.* move up the value chain) into your industry.

5   BARGAINING POWER OF CUSTOMERS

Powerful buyers use their size and importance to negotiate price down, or quality and service up, by playing industry rivals against each other. Buyers have power when they purchase in large volumes relative to a vendor's size, when vendor industries have high fixed costs, or when products are highly standardized. Buyers can also threaten to backward integrate. Amazon is working on building its own delivery network in order to contain shipping costs. This will take business away from their current suppliers such as UPS, FedEx and the US Postal Service.

When buyers do not have power, they sometimes organize to gain power. Group purchasing organizations are a structured effort to aggregate demand to negotiate better pricing.

Porter recommends developing strategies to i) take advantage of the changes in the forces; ii) gain more leverage to claim a higher percent of the profit; or iii) serve a market segment where the forces are weakest. By understanding customer needs and technology trends, you can identify their impact on the forces within your industry. Depth strategies are a way to gain power with customers. Scale strategies and standardizing inputs allow you to improve your bargaining position with suppliers. Innovation strategies, along with leadership or value differentiation strategies, are a way to avoid pure price competition with rivals. Niching lets you focus on a segment of the market where industry forces are weakest.

9.2. Portfolio Analysis

Consolidation is part of any market as it matures. Your rivals may be integrating cells on the market map to gain additional bargaining power with suppliers or with customers (see Chapter 10). It is also critical to understand how competitors are consolidating within a market space to gain share, and how that will impact the attractiveness of your product offering.

The good news is that relative market share does not correlate as strongly with profitability as it once did. [67] In a 2014 update to the BCG Growth Matrix, new research by BCG shows market share leadership is not as critical as when Bruce Henderson first introduced the matrix in 1970.[68] The original logic was that high relative market share led to superior returns because of cost advantages from scale and experience. Henderson captured this relationship in a four-quadrant matrix that could be used to evaluate business units or product portfolios (FIGURE 9.2):

1   **CASH COWS:** low-growth, high-share business areas that should be milked for profits to fund the growth of stars.

---

67   Relative market share is calculated by dividing your market share by your largest competitor's market share.
68   This discussion on the BCG Growth Matrix is based on "The Growth Share Matrix" by Martin Reeves, Sandy Moose, and Thijs Venema, Perspectives, 2014

2   **STARS**: high-growth, high-share business areas that need cash to fuel growth

3   **QUESTION MARKS**: high-growth, low-share business areas that should be further invested in or divested based on their potential to become a star.

4   **PETS (FORMERLY DOGS)**: low-growth, low-share business lines that are unlikely ever to generate cash and should be divested or repositioned.

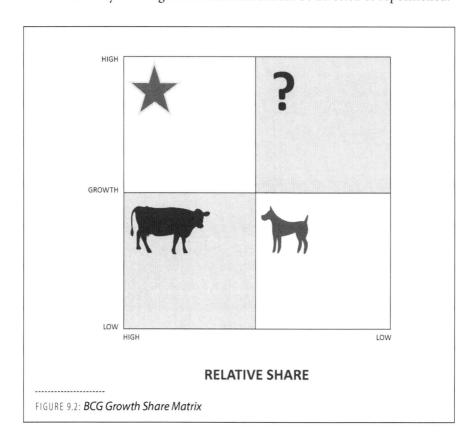

RELATIVE SHARE

FIGURE 9.2: *BCG Growth Share Matrix*

The purpose of the matrix was to guide businesses in creating a balanced portfolio and allocation of resources between mature product lines to exploit and new high-growth opportunities to explore. As markets have sped up, a company's ability to adapt to change, or drive change, has become just as important for achieving competitive advantage as market share was when the matrix was introduced.

BCG's new analysis shows that companies cycle business lines between the quadrants twice as fast as previously, decreasing from four years in 1992 to two years in 2012. The relative share of profits from cash cows is down from 53% in 1982 to 40% in 2012, while share of profits from stars jumped from 6% to 22% during the same time period. The matrix now needs to be applied at a faster cadence with more emphasis on strategic experimentation. Companies need to devote more resources to continually exploring new markets, business models, and product areas to remain competitive, while also learning to do so faster and with greater economy.

BCG recommends that companies:

1   Increase the number of question marks. Test them rapidly. Create a culture that encourages risk taking and tolerates failure.
2   Milk cows efficiently through incremental innovation to keep them performing and increasing profitability.
3   Keep pets on a short leash. Use pets to capture failure signals and extract as much value as possible before divestment.
4   Keep a balanced portfolio of stars that will become cows and fund new question marks that will become tomorrow's stars.

Navigating the growth matrix is complex. Product managers play a central role in supporting our organization's efforts to rapidly test ideas, incrementally innovate, and capture failure signals. Strategic experimentation and frequent adaptation are the norm. Key concepts for analyzing our situation and performing these tasks are covered in Chapters 6: Creating Product-Market Fit and Chapter 7: Purposeful Learning. Agile methods are a further component for achieving rapid learning and cost-effective exploration. Successfully applying Agile for competitive advantage is the topic of this book's companion, *Agile Excellence for Product Managers.*

9.3 Connected Devices Case Study

As we discuss industry analysis, it is worth noting that we are in a new wave of technology innovation and adoption that will increase rivalry, and which may again favor size. Michael Porter in his Nov 2014 Harvard Business Review article "How Smart, Connected Products are Transforming Competition" characterizes the current situation as the third wave of IT Driven Competition. The first wave came in the 1960s and 1970s with the automation of individual tasks such as order processing. The second wave came in the 1980s and 1990s with the Internet, which allowed companies to integrate their operations and supply chains with, and across, geographies, suppliers, and customers. In each of the previous two waves, products remained relatively unchanged. In this third wave, IT is being embedded directly into the product with sensors, software, and connectivity (the so called "Internet of Things" or IOT).

Connected devices can send a constant stream of data back to the manufacturer or service providers about their status, allowing a proactive relationship between provider and customer. Data collected by these devices can be analyzed to identify patterns of failure — and, ultimately, fixes can be pushed out to the devices to prevent a problem from occurring or recurring. Products can continue to be improved after they are in use. Tesla has differentiated itself in the auto industry for improving its automobile every few months with automatic updates to the software. Enhancements have included autopilot with improvements based on data collected from millions of miles of real driving, a feature that keeps the interior temperature cool while the car is unoccupied, and updates to the media player and dashboard interface. Similarly, in the consumer electronics space, the Amazon Echo digital assistant speaker, and the cloud platform that sits behind it, allows the product's voice recognition ability to be regularly improved based on usage and for new skills to be released regularly.

Industry Boundaries are on the Move.

Home lighting, audio and video, climate control, and security have traditionally been four separate industries. Now they exist within the larger industry of home automation. Because there are benefits to integrating these four areas and unifying their control, rivalry will increase and better-capitalized companies will be better able to invest in developing the new infrastructure and IT capabilities to compete.

In a related situation, it would have seemed unlikely that an e-commerce, search, and software company would ever find themselves in direct competition in a major market. Yet that is exactly the situation that Amazon, Google, and Microsoft find themselves in as I write this book. All three compete to provide the underlying infrastructure for the delivery of cloud services.

Porter also identifies four levels of capabilities for connected products that build on each other: Monitoring, Control, Optimization, and Autonomy (FIGURE 9.3).

The Product-as-a-Service model has arrived and has many implications for products, service delivery, business models, and industries. Manufacturers may now have an ongoing relationship with their customers and require DevOps groups, just as Software-as-a-Service (SaaS) companies do. Data analytics is another new function that manufacturers will need to master. All this change creates strategic challenges and opportunities that product managers must help their companies to solve, including understanding what is required to support these new products, how to best use the data, and whether to promote industry or proprietary standards.

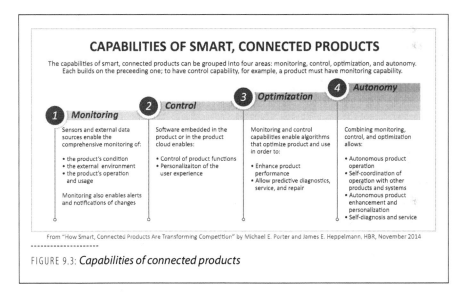

FIGURE 9.3: *Capabilities of connected products*

Wrap-up

Porter's Five Forces analysis allows you to understand the pressures on the different players in your industry. By monitoring the trends across the value chain, you can anticipate where the industry will move, and adjust your strategy to remain competitive on an ongoing basis. Furthermore, the third wave of IT-driven competition presents a special opportunity to improve your competitive position through superior strategy and execution.

CHAPTER 10

Mapping
Your Markets

A Market Map is a flexible visualization tool that I developed in the late 1990s. The map plots areas of the market space in which your company and your competitors participate. I usually divide the map into market segments and product areas (FIGURE 10.1). Thinking back to the basic strategy frameworks introduced in Chapter 8, if a company occupies many market segments across one or two product areas, it is following a scale strategy. If the company's offering spans many product areas in a single market segment, it is pursuing a depth strategy. If the company occupies a single market and product area, or unrelated market and product areas, it is an innovator. One can also create maps that only explore a single market, and the axis would be product area vs. product area using different dimensions for each axis. Even sub-segments within a market can be represented — such as low end, mid-tier, and premium to highlight how a company competes.

SCALE STRATEGY		MARKET SEGMENTS			
Product Areas	I	II	III	IV	V
A					
B					
C					
D					

DEPTH STRATEGY		MARKET SEGMENTS			
Product Areas	I	II	III	IV	V
A					
B					
C					
D					

INNOVATION STRATEGY		MARKET SEGMENTS			
Product Areas	I	II	III	IV	V
A					
B					
C					
D					

T-STRATEGY		MARKET SEGMENTS			
Product Areas	I	II	III	IV	V
A					
B					
C					
D					

FIGURE 10.1: *Four common strategy patterns*

Recall from Chapter 1 that two of the five elements to analyze when creating your product strategy are the strategies of your business and your competitors. First, your plan needs to align with your business's strategy and its ability to fund and support your recommendation. Second, markets are dynamic. Your competitors will be executing their strategies at the same time. Your analysis must account for their actions and anticipate how they may respond to your plans. Market Maps help you visualize the strategies that your company and your competitors are following.

Rarely does a company's map look so perfect as to match one of the patterns in figure 10.1. Companies are opportunistic, or may inherit product areas with an acquisition that they otherwise would not have pursued. Still, if you understand the weight of each cell (*i.e.* how important that cell is to the company's business) on the map, the underlying strategy will emerge. You will be able to identify market spaces that a company will fiercely defend or more easily surrender. In the end, you want to understand both *where* and *how* a company is likely to compete.

10.1 Creating the Map

During the time that I have been creating market maps, I have learned there is some art in getting the correct granularity. If the map is too detailed, it becomes hard to read and maintain; if it takes too broad an overview, it will not illuminate the ways different companies approach the market.

When starting a map, i) ensure that it covers an area larger than that in which you compete today (this allows you to see the adjacencies and identify opportunities as well as places of vulnerability); ii) capture your strategy and the competitors you want to track (It should include areas where you or your competitors have a product offering); and iii) for each company, shade the cells in the map where that company participates.

For companies with multiple business units, map only the business units that touch the market segment of interest or in which there is shared synergy and planning. For example, if I created a market map for Netflix, I would include HBO because the HBO GO service is a direct competitor. I would be less likely to include HBO's parent company, Time Warner. Although for some analyses, including Time Warner would be relevant because of the potential synergies between all of Time Warner's media assets. Looking at another example, if I competed against Honeywell in the home market (*e.g.* thermostats or home security), I would not map the market segments Honeywell occupies in the Oil and Gas industry. Honeywell's Oil and Gas business unit shares little in common with its Home business unit, having different customers, distribution, sales and marketing, operations, and research and development groups.

10.2 Analyzing Market Maps

Accurately interpreting a map requires additional data overlays and context:

1   **REVENUE:** over their history, companies make opportunistic moves in addition to strategic moves. They even get pulled into product areas by existing customers that they might otherwise not choose to serve. To separate these from their core business, you have to look at revenue. Where does the company make the majority of its sales? I have seen maps where a company appears to cover a broad area of the market yet, on further inspection, generates 80% of its revenue from a single product line and market segment.

2   **WHERE TO COMPETE:** market maps excel at showing where a company competes. Evaluate each company's map to see which of the three basic strategies the company is following. If the shaded area is T-shaped, it may be pursuing scale in its primary product area and also going deep in its main market segment. Most likely, the intersection of product and market is the heart of this company. It is their stronghold, commanding the most resources and driving their product development budgets. It represents the market area they will defend most vigorously. Ask yourself where the best places are for you to expand? What about your competition?

3   **HOW TO COMPETE:** does the company compete on cost, value or leadership? What is its business model? Is the company high touch or low touch? Some whole product dimensions such as support, professional services, and outsourced services can be included on the map. Keep in

mind that although you may occupy the same cell on the map, you may serve different customer segments.

4   **MARKET TRENDS**: How large is the market in each cell? How quickly is it growing or shrinking? What are the regulatory trends? What are the economic trends? What are the demographic trends?

5   **TECHNOLOGY TRENDS**: what technology trends are impacting your market? Which areas of the map are susceptible to technology driven disruption? Will the technology shift place you in competition with companies that previously served a different segment of the market?

6   **SUPPLIER CONSOLIDATION**: Is the market mature? Are suppliers consolidating and gaining more power? How does this impact margins?

7   **CUSTOMER CONSOLIDATION**: has the industry been consolidating? Are there fewer, but larger accounts to sell to? Do you need to broaden your offering to serve them better? Are there different product areas that a customer should logically purchase together?

8   **NEW ENTRANTS**: who are the innovators, occupying a single cell of the map, who may threaten your market position?

9   **MARKET POSITION**: are you the market leader? Are you a follower? Is there an axis of competition on which you can differentiate?

10 **PRIMACY IN ACCOUNT**: of all the solutions in a customer's account that need to integrate with each other, which one is the most important to running their organization? Which solution do they typically purchase first? Which solution commands the most resources and budget from the organization? Having primacy affects your power in an account and your ability to set standards or follow standards.

11 **ECONOMIES OF SCALE**: which solutions and value chain functions should be combined? Is scale most valuable in operations, sales and marketing, or research and development? What is the minimum scale to participate in a value chain area?

12 **COMPETITIVE TRENDS:** how is consolidation occurring in your industry? Is consolidation occurring through forward or backward integration in the value chain or across market segments (*i.e.* horizontally)? How does industry consolidation affect your strategy, and how do you need to adjust to remain competitive?

13 **COMPETITORS:** which cells on the market map are most important to own? Which will be the most contested? What will your competitors' market maps look like in 3–5 years? Where are your competitors' strong, vulnerable, or inflexible?

14 **COMPETITIVE RESPONSE:** how will your competitors likely respond to your planned moves in the marketplace?

10.3 Evolving Markets Case Study

A healthcare company I worked with pursued a depth strategy that offered everything necessary for a single, surgical specialty. The business sold equipment, tools, and devices and had knowledgeable representatives that helped educate surgeons on the use of the products and the latest surgical techniques. It was a successful strategy for many years. Then hospitals started consolidating. To manage costs, they centralized purchasing, reduced vendors, and drove standardization across clinical areas and the operating room. Hospitals increased their bargaining power. Large manufacturers pursuing scale strategies were best equipped to meet the needs of this more powerful customer. Johnson and Johnson and US Surgical had the most competitive bids for disposables such as sutures and staples. The general surgeons drove the equipment choices and favored companies that could fully outfit a multi-specialty operating room. Equipment manufacturers such as Stryker had the advantage. We also struggled to remain competitive in some areas in our product portfolio because of our lower volumes. The simplified markets maps in figure 10.2 show how the needs of the hospital came to be fully met through two or three of our competitors, because our surgical specialty had less influence in the purchasing decision.

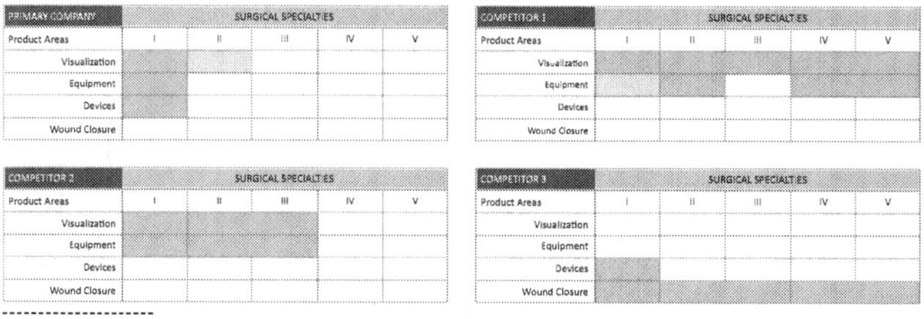

FIGURE 10.2: *Market maps demonstrate how two or three competitors replace my client's solution*

The company had two options: merge or pivot. A new growth market had been opening up: surgical centers. As the hospital market consolidated, entrepreneurial physicians set-up focused surgical centers. The centers specialized on a narrow set of procedures that could be performed in higher volume and at lower costs than in a general hospital. In the surgical center market, the company's ability to be a one-stop shop for a single specialty was once again valued, and the business unit remained independent.

Wrap-up

Market Maps provide a powerful visualization tool to compare companies' strategies for deciding where to compete. By overlaying additional data, a fuller story emerges. Market Maps also provide important context for SWOT and industry analysis. The maps make strengths, weaknesses, opportunities, and threats easier to see, as well as highlight how some elements of industry consolidation are occurring. Lastly, Market Maps give visibility to opportunities and threats outside your current product areas and make apparent adjacent market areas that would fit well into your product portfolio.

CHAPTER 11

Pricing for Competitive Advantage

P ricing your product or service is a key strategic decision. It requires serious thought and should be considered in the discovery phase of exploring and validating an opportunity (and then revisited throughout the product lifecycle). Price plays a central role both in your recommendation to management to fund product development and when working with Engineering on the design and feature set to optimize value while managing costs. Furthermore, your pricing strategy will influence your roadmap and your plans to maximize returns throughout the product lifecycle. Nevertheless, we as product managers are often more comfortable managing the feature set, and can overlook how critical price is to the success of our products.

At its most effective, your pricing model provides your product and business with a durable competitive advantage. We saw this when Netflix employed subscription pricing to carve out a protected position in the market to develop its DVD mail order business, knowing Blockbuster, with its transactional model and reliance on late fees, would not be able to easily match. But even if you select a similar pricing model as your competitors, understanding your strategy and your competitors' businesses will enable you to effectively anticipate and respond to your competitors' moves in the marketplace.

11.1 Three Factors of Pricing

The right features at too high a price can kill a product. Alternately, your product may appear to be successful, your sales volume is at the level planned, but you have actually set the price of your product too low, leaving money on the table and limiting your ability to invest in the future. There are three factors that influence the price you can command for your product: value to customer, competitive intensity, and costs.

Pricing starts with understanding the value your product delivers to the customer (i.e. the problem your product solves for the customer). To be more specific, you need to understand the value your product delivers for each customer segment, as perceived by those customers. Your goal is to target each segment with an offering that matches that segment's perceived value of solving the problem and its importance. This allows you to maximize topline revenue for the product in aggregate. This is easier for some products than others. Airlines successfully charge travelers different prices for the exact same product, the flight from Point A to Point B, since a trip has a different value to each passenger. Passengers are not well-informed about what others on the plane paid for their seat and tolerate this situation. This technique is known as yield management. Other methods to segment pricing include offering different configurations (basic, better, best), tier-based pricing based on volume or usage, and bundles. All are ways to align your offering with the needs and willingness to pay of different customer segments.

Competitive intensity limits the price you can charge. If you charge too much, your pricing will attract new entrants. This effect is why identifying durable differentiation for your offering is such a significant strategic consideration. The more you can differentiate your product in the eyes of the customer, by segment, the more pricing power you have, even in a highly competitive market.

Last, *costs* matter. Although, costs should never be the sole determinant of price, they are a constraint. The costs to develop, product, market, sell, and support a product are all critical factors in determining what product opportunities and markets to pursue. Further, your ability to manage your costs without compromising customer value gives you greater flexibility in pricing, addressing competitors, and achieving your business goals.

11.2 Product Goals and Pricing Strategies

When establishing your pricing, or when periodically reviewing and potentially revising it, you need to first identify your market situation and short and long-term goals for your product. In general, you can optimize for profit, revenue or market share. You have to pick one. There are three basic pricing strategies from which to start: Penetration, Skimming, and Maximization.

Penetration pricing is when a company prices a product low relative to its value. This does not mean the product is inexpensive. Toyota used penetration pricing to enter the luxury car market when it launched its Lexus brand. The goal of penetration pricing is to grab market share at the expense of revenue and profit. Penetration pricing is recommended when barriers to switching are high or when there is upsell opportunity to increase the lifetime value of the customer. Freemium pricing strategies are a version of this pricing strategy. Penetration pricing is also a good option when there are network effects (where the value of the product increases with the number of users). Social networks and technology platforms are examples of products whose value increases the more people who use them. Lastly, penetration pricing works well when the additional sales volume allows you to lower your costs and preserve your margin. The risk with penetration pricing is that your competitors will match your price, starting a price war. Thus, it is best used when you have a resource or cost advantage over the competition.

Skim pricing is when a company targets a segment of the market with a high willingness to pay, favoring high margins over volume. It makes sense to pursue a skimming strategy when the profit of selling to a small, price insensitive segment of the market outweighs selling at a lower price and higher volume to a larger market. This is often the case with products with high variable costs. Skim pricing works in the luxury goods market as a way to create exclusivity, by placing the product out of reach of most customers. Patent protection can also create an environment for skim pricing. As a reader of this book, you are more likely to employ something known as *sequential skim pricing*. This is when you target an initial group of price-insensitive customers and then lower the price to address an increasingly larger share of the market. This strategy works well to balance supply and demand if supply is limited while your company ramps-up production capacity. Apple followed this approach with the iPhone. The 8 GB model sold for $599 when it launched in June 2007 and the price dropped to $399 three months later.[69] 12 months later, the next generation iPhone was priced at $199.[70] You can also launch a higher-end product followed by a lower-end product.

Maximization is when a company focuses on optimizing total profit or revenue. Your price is selected to achieve the desired result based on the point in the price elasticity[71] curve where revenue or profit is maximized. This strategy means your product will be priced with the pack. Based on the product's perceived value and differentiation, it could be priced on the high side, the low side, or in the middle relative to the competition. But the product is not so differentiated as to be able to support skim pricing nor conditions correct to justify penetration pricing.

11.3 What to Charge — Assessing Value to the Customer

Through your Voice of Customer (VOC) research program you should already be understanding the customer needs and segmentation (i.e. groups of customers with shared priorities and needs.) During these discussions, you should also ask customers about how they value a set of needs. When you have a concept (with a feature set) two questions I ask to determine pricing bounds are:

1   At what price would the product be so INEXPENSIVE you would question its quality?
2   At what price would the product be so EXPENSIVE that on price alone, you would not consider purchasing it?

You should also ask purchase intent at a given price point on a scale of 1–5 where 1 = no interest in purchasing this product and 5 = I want to purchase this product today. A good rule of thumb is 50% of fives and 10%-20% of fours will actually buy.[72]

----

69   This steep price drop in such a short period of time created an outcry from customers and customers received $100 credit toward other Apple products.
70   http://blogs.harvard.edu/dlarochelle/2010/01/14/iphone-price-history/
71   Price elasticity describes how the product's unit sales varies with a corresponding change in the product's price.
72   *Monetizing Innovation* by Madhavan Ramanujam and Georg Tacke (2016, John Wiley & Sons, Inc.), p. 47.

Lastly, ask for a commitment. A few different ways include having the customer agree to be notified when the product is available, answer additional questions about the product, or place a pre-order. For example, if *all* the participants who indicated their intent to purchase was five wanted to be notified when the product was available, I would be more confident in their interest. On the flip side, if *none* of the participants that indicated their intent to purchase was five wanted to be contacted when the product was available, my confidence in their interest would decrease. No commitment likely means no interest, or that at least some issue is preventing successful product-market fit. I would conduct follow-on research to get a better grasp of the desirability of the product.

In Chapter 7: Purposeful Learning, there is a case study for a consumer product where the company did a concept test survey as one of the key tests in their question chain. FIGURE 11.1 shows how willingness to pay varied with price in the context of that survey.

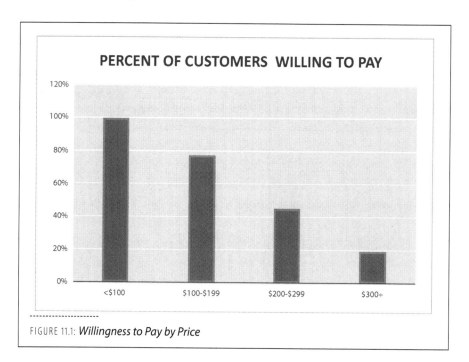

FIGURE 11.1: *Willingness to Pay by Price*

This was the product team's first look at how willingness to pay changed the price of the offering or how sales volume might change based on the price (*i.e.* price elasticity). Elasticity is usually negative. Thus, as price increases, volume decreases. A price elasticity of -1.5 would mean that a 10% increase in price would result in a 15% decrease in sales. Price elasticity varies significantly at different price points.[73]

$$\epsilon = \frac{\text{\% change in unit sales}}{\text{\% change in price}}$$

FIGURE 11.2: *Price Elasticity Formula*

In the example in figure 11.1, the elasticity between a price that is less than $100 versus between $100 and $200 is -0.16, a relatively low elasticity. Customers became increasingly price sensitive with an elasticity of -1.42, as the price goes above $200.[74] At a minimum, the data in the example gives us important initial guidance on how to price this product and whether to invest in further research on basic and premium offerings to capture the less price sensitive, high-end and the more price sensitive, low-end segments of the market.

In addition to judging willingness to pay, you also need to understand the value customers place on different features and services. There are a number of methods you can implement, without the need for a professional research firm, to assist in making informed pricing and product feature decisions. One technique is to ask customers to sort features in order importance. Another method is to ask customers to spend $100 on the features on which they want your company to focus, or have customers "buy" features from a list with prices to configure the product they want at a price point they are willing to pay. These methods will provide insight into the features that customers (by segment) value the most.

73   The discussion and formula are from *The Strategies and Tactics of Pricing* by Thomas T. Nagle and Reed K. Holden (Prentice-Hall, Inc., 1995) pp. 100–101.
74   The data in figure 11.1 has been aggregated to simplify the example and make it easier to read. In the actual survey, the participants specified a price so the actual data was more granular than the $100 price bands being compared in this example.

They will also let you determine the features that customers do not value and therefore should be eliminated from the product plan.[75]

11.4 How to Charge — Selecting the Optimal Unit of Value

Deciding how to charge is equally important as deciding what to charge. The unit of value used to price your product is fundamental to your business model. How you are going to price for, and capture, value is a key product strategy decision.

Characteristics of an effective pricing structure are:

1   Easy to explain and understand
2   Matches the value the customer receives from the product
3   Measurable to enable reporting and billing
4   Customer can manage their expense and avoid surprises
5   Future proof to allow the capture of customer upside without renegotiating the contract

With the advent of connected devices as described in Chapter 9: Anticipating the Future with Industry Analysis, many companies can expect to have ongoing relationships with their customers. Let's look at some examples that rank highly on all five characteristics, with a focus on recurring revenue models.

Customer relationship management:
applying users as a proxy for value
Salesforce.com charges per user and supports four versions of its product with different capabilities suitable for small teams through to large organizations. At the time of this writing, subscriptions range from $75/user/month to $300/user/month based on the subscription level selected. Salesforce.com is employing users as a proxy for value. Thus, the more users a company has on the solution, the more value the company derives.

---

[75]   If you have budget to hire a market research firm you might also consider adaptive conjoint analysis and MaxDiff analysis. In this chapter, my goal is to arm you with the tools that you can implement yourself on a regular basis.

Insightly.com is a simpler CRM system solution that competes with Salesforce in the small business segment. The company's plans range from $12/user/month for the basic solution to $99/user/month for their most advanced capabilities. Similar to Salesforce.com, Insightly charges per user. Since Insightly uses price to differentiate itself from Salesforce.com, by using the established per user pricing model, customers can easily compare between options.

Legal services: segmenting by service level
LegalZoom offers legal services, such as business incorporation, amendments, trademark, etc. The services, which are inexpensive for legal work, are provided for a fixed fee within a guaranteed time frame. The company upsells priority turnaround. Customers who need the work done faster pay upwards of 75% more. LegalZoom segments customers by the urgency of their need. This allows the company to better manage its costs to enable it to offer basic legal services at a great value.

Genomic data: matching the pricing model to the market segment
DNAnexus provides a cloud platform for sharing, analyzing, and managing genomic data. The company targets two markets: researchers and genomic test providers. Each market has its own distinct pricing model. Research customers pay for data storage and analysis time. Test providers pay per test. The pricing models map well to how DNAnexus adds value and the needs of the customer to manage their costs. Researchers pay for usage, since it is hard to predict how and when their research might lead to a valuable insight. Test providers pay per test, which is the unit of measure by which they charge for their services. By paying for each test, the provider's expense scales linearly with its business volume. This allows them to easily manage their costs.

Medical equipment: razor and blade model for capital equipment
Intuitive Surgical develops robotic systems to assist surgeons in performing minimally invasive surgery. The company has three primary revenue sources: the robot, an annual service agreement, and instruments and accessories used per procedure. In 2015, the split of revenue from these three sources was 30%, 20%, and 50% respectively.[76] 70% of Intuitive Surgical's revenue is recurring, with half tracking directly to usage by the customer.

----

76   Intuitive Surgical Investor Presentation Q4 2016.

Home security cameras: positioning against the competition

A young market in the home security space is for wireless video cameras with cloud storage. Let's look at three companies that participate in the market — Nest, Netgear and Ring — to see how they price and position against each other (table 11.1).

Nest is the premium offering and captures the highest value in recurring, subscription revenue through its cloud storage service. Netgear positions below Nest, selling the camera and employing a freemium strategy for cloud storage. Netgear's strategy is to acquire customers by giving away basic cloud storage and then upsell them to a longer term of storage. Ring differentiates with its core offering of a video doorbell that users can answer from their smartphones, and which can record motion events (storing continuous video requires significantly more disk space than motion events). Ring supplements its system with motion-triggered security cameras (basically the video doorbell without the button) for additional monitoring around one's home. Ring places most of its value in the hardware, which it prices on par with Nest. The company charges substantially less than its competitors for cloud storage, at $3/device/mo for 180 days of motion events.

MANUFACTURER	CAMERAS	VIDEO DOORBELL	DAYS OF CLOUD STORAGE	RECORDING	MOTION ALERTS	TALK AND LISTEN	RESOLUTION	POWER	ONE TIME	RECURRING
Nest Outdoor Camera	3	NA	30	Continuous	Yes	Yes	1080p HD	Hardwired	$597	$60/mo
Netgear Arlo	3	NA	30	Continuous	Yes	No	720p HD	Hardwired	$516	$40/mo
Netgear Arlo	3	NA	30	Motion Events Only	Yes	No	720p HD	Battery	$450	$10/mo
Netgear Arlo	3	NA	7	Motion Events Only	Yes	No	720p HD	Battery	$450	*free*
Ring	2	1	180	Motion Events Only	Yes	Yes	720p HD	Battery	$597	$9/mo

Pricing and configurations as of December 2016.

TABLE 11.1: *Pricing plans for wireless home security cameras*

Online advertising: letting the market set the price through auction

The first pricing models for online advertising charged marketers per 1000 impressions (CPM). This model mapped well to traditional print and broadcast media that advertisers understood well. Later, more performance driven-models emerged, such as cost per click (CPC) and cost per action (CPA), that took advantage of the trackability of behavior in the online world. When Google started to monetize its search page by placing sponsored links alongside search results and later syndicating ads on other web properties, the company knew the system had to be automated to scale. Google could never expect to negotiate deals with every buyer and sellers. At the same time, if it had set fixed prices for inventory, it would have left money on the table. So instead their management selected an auction model. Marketers bid on key words alongside which their ads are placed. The advertiser only pays Google when a user clicks through. Google further optimizes advertising placement or yield based on the bid amount and the frequency with which users click on that advertisement. This optimizes revenue to Google and ensures that each user sees the most relevant ads.

Industrial equipment: power-by-the-hour

In 1962, Rolls-Royce launched 'power-by-the-hour' maintenance plans that charged airline operators a fixed cost per hour of engine operation. Airline operators want a working engine. They do not want to be managing spare parts. Since costs to operate an engine correlates to usage, power-by-the-hour programs allow airlines a predictable level of expense to maintain their engines that adjusts to their business volume. Since 1962, the program has been improved to include engine monitoring to predict failure and schedule maintenance prior to an unplanned event.[77] Compared to fee-for-service maintenance plans, Rolls-Royce's decision to charge by usage aligns their interests with their customers, since both benefit from reduced downtime.

There are many different ways to charge for your product or service. The above examples demonstrate different pricing models that companies have chosen to maximize value capture over time and better serve their customers. How you charge for your product is a key pricing strategy decision that is as important, if not more important, than what you charge because it is easier to adjust your price than to change your pricing model.

---

77 http://www.rolls-royce.com/media/press-releases/yr-2012/121030-the-hour.aspx

11.5 Contribution Margin and Breakeven Curves

In addition to understanding the relationship between price and volume (*i.e.* price elasticity), you also need to understand how a pricing decision impacts profitability. Breakeven curves provide a way to visualize the trade-off between elasticity and profitability (FIGURE 11.3). The curve maps how volume needs to adjust for a given price change to maintain constant profitability. With a breakeven curve, you do not need to know the exact price elasticity for your product. This simplifies the analysis since you most likely do not have the precise numbers. Rather, the curve sets the bounds for the minimum and maximum elasticity of demand to justify a pricing decision.[78] It allows you to evaluate how realistic the desired volume change is and whether a price change will be profitable.

Before exploring breakeven curves, we must first understand contribution margin. Contribution margin is the money left over *after all incremental costs have been subtracted from each additional unit sold*. Thus, contribution margin is the money that is available to cover the fixed and sunk costs[79] of the organization. After subtracting all these costs, any additional money left over is true profit. To maximize profitability, you maximize contribution margin. This decision is independent of fixed and sunk costs.

Incremental costs often equal variable costs, but there are times when increasing or decreasing volume will raise or lower one of these costs in a non-linear way. At one company I worked for, the service delivery relied on data analysts. As new customers signed up, our excess analyst capacity shrunk. Once the company reached capacity, servicing the next new customer would require a new analyst to be hired. This represented a large incremental cost attributable to that sale. Similarly, in manufacturing, there is tooling capacity that, once exceeded, can trigger an incremental, capital expense. On the flip side, sometimes adding volume allows a company to lower costs. For example, a company may be able to negotiate better terms for parts or services.

----

78 *The Strategies and Tactics of Pricing* by Thomas T. Nagle and Reed K. Holden (Prentice-Hall, Inc., 1995) p. 53.
79 Sunk costs are non-recoverable costs and should not be considered in future investment decision making.

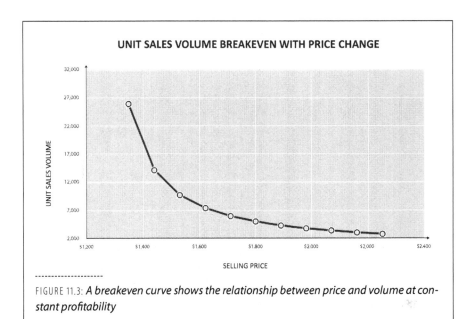

FIGURE 11.3: *A breakeven curve shows the relationship between price and volume at constant profitability*

I was once presented with an interesting puzzle by a client in the medical devices space. Because medical devices are regulated, manufacturers can charge substantially different prices for their products in different geographies without fear of the customers purchasing the product in one country and shipping it to another. In our case, a competitor significantly dropped their price on a product in South America. They appeared to be pursuing an aggressive penetration strategy. My client instinctively wanted to "go to war" and undercut their competitor's price.

Fortunately, my client's management decided that we should take time to analyze the situation before we responded. It turned out that my client purchased a component of their solution from an original equipment manufacturer (OEM), whereas the competitor developed and manufactured that part of the solution themselves. My client, therefore, effectively had zero sunk or fixed costs. Instead, my client's costs were 100% variable and the component we sourced from the OEM was relatively expensive, because, baked into the price the OEM charged us, was their i) research and development; ii) a portion of the capital expenditures of running a manufacturing operation; and iii) a markup. The competitor, in contrast, had high fixed and sunk costs imposed by their in-house research and development and manufacturing capability but little incremental cost for each additional unit manufactured (FIGURE 11.4).

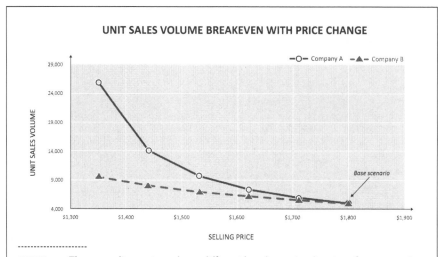

FIGURE 11.4: *The same discount can have different breakeven implications for companies based on contribution margin of each additional sale (Company A starting contribution margin = 31%. Company B starting contribution margin = 53%)*

Contrary to our initial belief, our competitor made a rational pricing decision based on their cost structure. Even at the lower price, they still had a generous contribution margin and would make a greater profit with a modest gain in volume. If my client matched the competitor's price, they would never recoup the lost margin on additional volume. My client, in other words, would be on the losing side of that price war.

There was little my client could do in the short term to address the actual cost advantage the competitor had in that product category. This meant that in a head-to-head sale, it did not make sense to match the competitor's price. But my client was able to bundle that product with other equipment to create a full solution. The combined contribution margin of the bundle allowed the company to provide an adequate discount to mitigate the competitor's price advantage on the standalone product.

11.6 Assembling your Pricing Strategy

Let's review the pieces of pricing and how to assemble them into a single strategy.

1   Research the three factors that impact your pricing strategy: value to customer, competitive intensity, and the costs of the solution. This research and analysis includes understanding customer segments, what each segment is willing to pay, what each segment values in the solution, and rough price elasticity within each segment. Bear in mind that you will never have "perfect" information or "precise" answers.

2   Select your goals and set your pricing strategy. What does this product need to achieve for the company? What pricing strategy will best meet your company's short and long-term objectives? What basic pricing strategy — penetration, skimming, or maximization — should you use to develop your specific strategy?

3   Determine what to charge and the value that can be captured from each segment.

4   Determine how to charge. How will you capture the value? How will it map to the way customers derive value from the solution? How much value is captured upfront or onetime, and how much is recurring?

5   Understand how changes in price impact profitability by analyzing contribution margin. Create breakeven curves to assist in the analysis.

The last part is to take the assembled pricing strategy and develop guidelines for how and when it can be adjusted. Plan in advance for likely competitive, market, and business driven scenarios. Decide how you will react to competitors' actions in the market place, especially deep discounting. Develop scenarios in case sales are moving slower than anticipated as well as moving faster. Will you raise prices if you are close to capacity? Are you able to bring capacity on quickly if needed? Lastly, what types of promotion, if any, is Marketing allowed to run, and what discount policy does Sales need to follow?

Once the product is in the market, you need to monitor its performance. With your pricing strategy in place, you will know how to react to dynamic market conditions, have the data to support your decision, and manage your product so it still meets the needs of the business.

PART III

Summary

This section covered a lot of ground. We learned basic strategies that companies follow and how to perform a SWOT analysis to assess companies' advantages and vulnerabilities. Porter's Five Forces helps us uncover the pressures acting on an industry and anticipate how the market will react. Market maps then provide a technique to visualize markets, company strategies, and a context for SWOT. The BCG growth matrix provides a framework for evaluating our product portfolio, with the new finding that speed now matters more than size. Lastly, identifying the correct price point and pricing strategy will strengthen our competitive position.

Applying the analyses in this section along with the five elements of product strategy discussed in Chapter 1 will define how your organization frames the strategy discussion. These analyses are your model of how the world works, what's important to the customer, your role in the marketplace, and how much of the market you need to monitor and track on an ongoing basis.

Based on your analyses and knowledge of the customer:

1 Where do you see opportunities and threats?
2 Are you allocating enough investment to exploring new opportunities that will become your next stars?
3 Is your vision achievable, relevant, and adequately differentiated?
4 What basic strategy do you want to build upon to develop your unique strategy for achieving your vision?

5   Does your business have the capabilities and competencies to execute on the strategy?

6   What does your solution offering need to look like three to five years from now?

7   Do you need to buy, build, or partner to achieve your three to five-year plan?

8   How will you navigate competitors' moves and anticipated responses to your actions?

9   How will you translate the above considerations to your strategic roadmap?

Further, although many of the questions above are focused three to five years out, you also have to focus on what you need achieve in the next 90 days, and what needs to be in your ordered product backlog. For a five-year plan, 90 days represents the first five percent of your plan. For a three year and 18-month plan, the first 90-days represents eight and sixteen percent of the plan respectively. What you accomplish in the first 90 days and every subsequent 90-day period matters when it comes to realizing your longer-term strategy. It is important to stay focused.

Strategy is a competitive advantage. Remember to update and stress test your models regularly. This ensures you expend resources doing more of the right things and less of the wrong things. You should always be prepared to revise as new information is learned, but a good rule of thumb is to evaluate the information quarterly and revisit the entire analyses more critically on an annual basis.

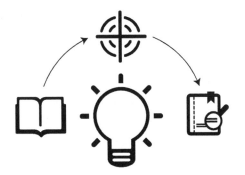

Conclusion

The Introduction of this book included a quote by Peter Drucker stating that strategic planning is "analytic thinking and commitment of resources to action" and warning that it is NOT "a box of tricks or bundle of techniques." Thus, the concepts presented in this book do not represent a linear path of analysis that, if followed, will produce the single, best answer. Rather, the methods and concepts covered in these pages are intended to help you create a model of how the world, in which your company and products compete, works. By performing the analysis to assemble your model (and ultimately testing and refining that model in the marketplace), you will generate the insights necessary to create a superior and defensible strategic plan.

This strategy will inform your vision and your roadmap. You will be confident your plan is achievable. Further, it will allow you truly to order your product backlog by business value, so that you may optimally commit the resources of your development team and company to action. This strategy will allow you to deliver value to your customers and win in the marketplace.

The strategy you create should also shift the discussion of how new opportunities and the "crisis *du jour*" are evaluated. It will help you make proactive investments in the future and avoid consuming all your resources purely reacting to events in the marketplace. When new information emerges that does not fit the model, the conversation centers around whether any part of the analysis is invalid. If so, update the strategy and re-evaluate your investments. If not, stay focused on executing your plan. Making deliberate choices is the difference between being a market leader or a market follower.

Assembling and maintaining all the facts, predictions, and insights that comprise a strategy is a lot of work, but it does make the job of the product manager easier once in place. To briefly summarize:

1. Strategy unifies product vision, roadmap, and backlog.
2. The five elements of product strategy are customer, market, competition, technology, and your business strategy.
3. Analyze the forces acting on your industry. Map your competitors to visualize their strategies, uncover their strengths and weaknesses, and anticipate their moves and reactions to your chosen plan.
4. Assess your product-market fit type. Are you an exploiter who can create a business case or an explorer who needs to be funded on a learning plan with a *key question chain*?
5. Understand how you will maintain growth across your portfolio of products.

Let us end the book with another quote by Peter Drucker, who said "management is doing things right; leadership is doing the right thing". Strategy is the work of leaders. It is difficult work. It is time-consuming work. It is about doing the right thing. Management is about the execution of one's strategy. It is about doing things right. To grow in your career as a product manager, you need not just to manage your product, but to lead your product. That journey starts with a great strategy.

Appendix A

Key Problem, Product Discovery and Business Model Questions

Many questions need to be validated. Below is a subset of the most basic ones. It's important to remember that, during any test of a hypothesis, you must remain open to the chance of discovering something unexpected, the sudden realization of an unanticipated insight, or the identification of a new path of inquiry.

Project

1   What are the business objectives of this project (measurable and timeline)?
2   How does the project support the corporate goals?
3   Are we the right company to bring this solution to market, and will we be able to compete effectively?

Problem

1   Who is the customer (be specific)?
   a   Who is the user?

    b   Who is the buyer? Are buyer and user the same person?

    c   Who influences the purchase, or is impacted by the purchase (answers might be an IT manager, a spouse, a child, etc.)?

    d   Who approves the purchase?

2   What problem does each of the customers want solved?

    a   State the problem.

    b   Describe the scenario when the problem is encountered.

    c   Do different segments exist with different needs (usage, behavioral, attitudes, or buying)?

    d   In considering the early product, which segments and users:

        i   Are most valuable?

        ii   Will the solution be optimized for?

        iii   Will the solution support?

        iv   Will the solution exclude?

3   What observational and/or numeric evidence has been collected to support how common and urgent the problem is?

    a   How do customers rank the importance of solving this problem?

    b   How do customers rank their current satisfaction with the current alternatives?

    c   What evidence exists that customers are willing to pay to solve this problem?

4   Do we believe there are enough customers willing to pay to solve this problem to constitute a market large enough to be worth pursuing?

Product

1   What are their current options for solving the problem (remember to include "do nothing")?

2   What are the strengths and weaknesses of those options? Remember to consider not just the product but also service, experience, ease of purchase, etc.

3   What is the market entry strategy?

    a   Are you entering an existing market with an optimized product?

    b   Are you creating a new market?

    c   Are you creating a new segment with a simpler, less expensive offering that targets users who currently are not being served by the existing solutions or whose needs are being overserved?

d   Are you targeting a niche market (i.e. optimized product for a narrow segment of market)?

4   What is the product solution?

a   What will the product look like?

b   How many configurations or models will be supported?

c   What functions will the product perform?

d   How do we want the user to feel when using the product?

e   What is the out of box experience?

f   How will customers learn to use the product?

g   What is the warranty?

5   Differentiation

a   How does our solution differ from the alternatives?

b   What is the level of differentiation? Is it:

    i   Incremental?

    ii   Major?

    iii Discontinuous?

d   Is the differentiation significant in the eyes of the customer?

a   Is the differentiation sustainable (IP, trade secret, exclusive distribution)?

6   What are the Solution/Development risks?

7   Who are the competitors?

a   What does the competitive landscape look like?

b   What are the likely competitive responses?

8   Are there any regulatory or legal issues to consider?

9   Are there any other open issues or risks?

Business Model

1   What are the key customer segments (ideal segments are measurable, reachable, stable and share the same needs and preferences)?

a   How will each segment be reached?

b   How will the customer be made aware of the solution?

c   Does the customer need to be educated about the solution (important for new markets)?

d   Do different segments require different channels for purchase and support?

e   Do different segments require different pricing models?

  f Do different segments require different service levels?

2 How will the product be monetized or priced?

  a What is the unit of value that will be sold?

  b What is the target price per unit of value (per user, per CPU, per gigabit, etc.)?

  c Are there multiple streams of revenue?

  d What services can be sold along with the product or vice versa (think beyond just warranty and support)?

3 Where will the product be found?

  a Where can the product be discovered?

  b Where can the product be purchased?

  c Where can the product be serviced?

4 Service experience — what level and type of service will customers receive when:

  a Learning about the product?

  b Purchasing the product?

  c Receiving support for the product?

  d Receiving training for the product?

5 Financials

  a How many qualified leads to generate a sale?

  b What is the target customer acquisition cost?

  c What is the target lifetime customer value?

  d What is the value chain for each channel?

  e What will your cost structure look like?

Appendix B

1 Product-Market Fit Case Studies

The case studies in this section are intended to illustrate companies that have successfully navigated each of the product-market fit types.[80] Product-market fit is only one of many factors a company needs to get right in order to succeed. Further, the case studies are provided as illustrations — there is no suggestion that the companies used explicitly iterative methods like those described in this book.

TYPE		OPTIMIZE (Type I)		MARKET DRIVEN (Type II)		TECH DRIVEN (Type III)		VISIONARY (Type IV)	
Problem		Defined	Defined	Defined	Defined	Undefined	Undefined	Undefined	Undefined
Solution	**Product**	Defined	Defined	Undefined	Undefined	Defined	Defined	Undefined	Undefined
	Business Model	Defined	Undefined	Defined	Undefined	Defined	Undefined	Defined	Undefined
Example		MS Word 2013	Dell	Flip	Hightail (formerly YouSendIt)	Gore Assoc.	Salesforce	Post-it® Notes	Xerox
		Samsung Galaxy				Vocera	Redbox		Twitter

TABLE 6.2: *Problem, product, and business model combine to yield eight different product-market fit challenges.*

---

80   The case studies in this section originally appeared in the ebook *Lean Product Management: Achieving Product-Market Fit in Record Time with Fewer Resources* by Greg Cohen (Silicon Valley: 280 Group Press, 2011). Some of the case studies have been slightly updated. A free copy of this original ebook is available for download in the resource section of www.agile-excellence.com

1.1 Optimizing (Type I)

Optimize (Type I)	Market Driven (Type II)
Tech Driven (Type III)	Visionary (Type IV)

Optimizing produces small levels of solution differentiation. Typically, these are products that are "new and improved" and, when combined with a new business model, sometimes have little feature-level product differentiation. When a market is no longer growing, optimizing is often the investment a company needs to make just to maintain its position in the marketplace.

Business Model Defined (examples: MS Word 2013 and Samsung Galaxy)

Because problem, solution, and business model are relatively well understood, it is possible for the product manager to create i) a reasonably accurate business case to describe an opportunity; and (ii) a market requirements document (MRD) to describe the prioritized needs of the user. The development team will be able to produce good estimates for the work needed to build the product if they have experience developing on the current codebase or hardware platform. The product marketing team will understand how to launch and promote the product and produce solid estimates of the likely revenue the company would achieve from its marketing investment. *Optimize* is where companies already in business spend most of their time. Short waterfall (*i.e.* serial development) methods can work well here. However, if the market is dynamic — requiring extra flexibility — or a short time to market has a large payoff, Agile development is preferred. Regardless, at the project level, the decision making cycle is linear and maps well to a traditional phase gate process.

MS WORD 2013 is an example of a product optimized over a period of two decades. At its release, it represented the next greatest version of the ubiquitous office application Word. It addressed bugs and issues uncovered by Word 2010 users and also included new features such a design tab to format documents, comment within comments for improved collaboration, and vastly improved border and table options. Microsoft had existing models to price and distribute the product, and could predict with good accuracy how it would sell. The next release, Word 2016, entered a less certain world and included business model changes, such as subscription pricing, and integration with Office 365 for online document management and collaboration.

The **SAMSUNG GALAXY** phone is a very different example. Samsung produced an optimized alternative to the Apple iPhone. Its major differentiating factor was that it was not an Apple product. It ran Android, a more open operating system and application ecosystem, and it cost less than the iPhone. Samsung pursued a fast follower strategy. Time to market was critical for Samsung to remain relevant in the phone market.

Business Model Undefined (example: Dell)

Pursuing a product optimizing strategy where the business model is undefined has the potential to create not just a successful product, but also a successful company. What is interesting about these companies is they often do it with products that lack meaningful differentiation. **Dell** originally sold a product called a "PC Clone". By its very definition, a clone is undifferentiated. What Dell did do was sell a good-quality product direct, with good service, competitive (although not the lowest) prices, and the ability for the customers to configure their systems exactly as they wanted them. Dell even offered risk-free return and next-day-at-home product assistance.[81] Dell further achieved competitive advantage through its superior supply chain management.[82]

1.2 Market Driven (Type II)

Business Model Defined (example: Flip Camera)

Optimize (Type I)	Market Driven (Type II)
Tech Driven (Type III)	Visionary (Type IV)

Pure Digital Technologies, creators of the Flip Camcorder, identified an under-served segment of the camcorder market and created a new category of camcorder called "shoot and share." At the time the Flip camera launched in 2007, camcorder sales were flat. Within a year of its introduction, Flip had 17% market share on a unit basis, four points behind Sony's 21% market leadership share. Flip camcorders were sold through a traditional retail channel.

---

81 http://content.dell.com/us/en/corp/our-story-company-timeline.aspx

82 Internal processes can provide companies with sustained competitive advantage. Some of these processes are within the influence of product managers, such as market research, others, such as supply chain management, are not. Agile development is a process that can be used for sustained competitive advantage.

Pure Digital Technologies used market insights to redefined the axes of competition (FIGURE B.1) in the marketplace. The traditional camcorder companies continued to improve areas that had long been satisfied, such as image quality and hours of storage. Flip cut way back on these (it was an inferior camera based on traditional measures) and instead focused on three under-served needs:

1   Ease of sharing video via email and the Internet
2   Ease of shooting with only five controls on the entire camera
3   Small size. The Flip camera wasn't just portable it was "pocketable".

FlipShare, the software for quick editing and sharing, was loaded onto the camcorder's solid state memory. A USB connector was built in (so there were no cables to carry or lose). When the camcorder was plugged into a computer, the editing and sharing software could be quickly installed. Lastly, the Flip camera was priced below a traditional camcorder.

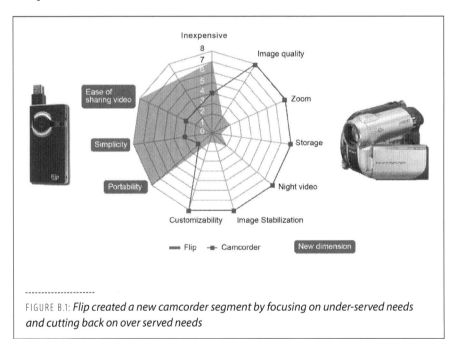

FIGURE B.1: *Flip created a new camcorder segment by focusing on under-served needs and cutting back on over served needs*

The fate of the Flip camcorder is worth further examination. Cisco Systems purchased Pure Digital Technologies in 2009 for $590 million in stock. Although still
enjoying strong sales and positive brand recognition, Cisco Systems announced
in 2011 that it was discontinuing the Flip camcorder line as part of a larger divestment of consumer focused products. One of the stated reasons was the threat
from smartphones, although Flip had a good many years left before smartphones
would make it obsolete.[83] Had Flip's management team explored new business
models, it might have positioned itself to take advantage of the smartphone
market. In particular, Flip might have built a subscription business around
FlipShare, offering consumers safe, cloud storage and easy sharing for their
memories. Once Flip users accumulated enough video on FlipShare, even if they
changed camcorders or moved to a smartphone, they may have stayed with the
FlipShare service. Another option would have been to pursue a niche strategy,
for example in what was, at that point, the small yet growing action segment that
GoPro now dominates.

Business Model Undefined (example:
hightail, formerly YousendIt)

In 2003, Ranjith Kumaran set out to address a market problem: it was difficult
for people to send large files via email and FTP. He founded YouSendIt and
developed an elegant solution, whereby a user could upload a file to YouSendIt
via the web and the recipient would receive an email with a link to download the
file. Senders and recipients whose email servers blocked large files, a common IT
practice in those days, found YouSendIt immediately useful.

The company, however, was unsure how to charge for their service. Had they looked
at the traditional delivery models, they would have charged per file delivered — just
as the post office charges per letter or package. But it must have struck Kumaran
that the established package delivery business model would not translate well to
electronic documents. The company experimented with advertising-based revenue but this did not generate enough income for two reasons. First, users go to
the YouSendIt site to either send or retrieve a file. They have a task on their mind
and don't linger on the site. They are unlikely to click on ads. Second, YouSendIt
has no way to work out a user's interests (the way, say, Google can by examining

---

83   http://en.wikipedia.org/wiki/Flip_camera

a search term, or a content site can match advertisements with an article), so advertisements could not be well targeted to the audience.

The company then explored a freemium model, in which the base service was free and higher value services required payment. YouSendIt sliced value along many dimensions, including total downloads per month and maximum file size; confirmed delivery; password protection; file expiration date controls; and the ability to send multiple files together. Users could subscribe to YouSendIt to get the premium features. A few of the premium features could be purchased on a per-transaction basis as well.

Later, YouSendIt developed business specific solutions. The core service largely stayed the same, but the business-specific offering was sold on a per-seat basis, and included custom branding and user level reporting. The company even became SAS70 Type II compliant. That isn't a benefit for individual users, such as creative professionals, but is important to enterprises and law firms using the YouSendIt solution.

While YouSendIt was growing to 50 million registered users, its market and competitive environment shifted. Deeply-funded competitors, such as Dropbox and Box, appeared. These new competitors had overlapping functionality with different business models, pricing, and value propositions. Nearly a decade into its life, YouSendIt needed a new strategy.

The company did deep customer research to identify a problem area it could dominate. With this research, management rebranded the company Hightail with a new focus on assisting advertising agencies and creative professional from idea creation to execution and final delivery. In the face of a challenging competitive environment in which it was unlikely to win, management went for a niching strategy (covered in section 8.3: Niching). Early results look promising.

1.3 Tech Driven (Type III)

In the tech driven category, companies select the solution, usually driven by a technological innovation, and then see where and how it can be applied.

Business Model Defined (example: Gore Associates and Vocera)

W. L. GORE & ASSOCIATES is a tech driven company. The company specializes in flouropolymers and constantly seeks to identify products that would be enhanced by their use. Gore is best known in the consumer market for Gore-Tex®, its semi-permeable fabric coating that is used to waterproof outerwear and footwear while remaining breathable and comfortable for the user. But they also produce products for the electronics, aerospace, automotive and medical industries, among others. Most companies would not seek to compete in such varied markets, but Gore is a technology-driven company. They start with the solution and identify problems, independent of industry, where they can apply their knowhow — a business model they have successfully been applying for over half a century.

VOCERA COMMUNICATIONS is a classic technology driven start-up. In 2000, the founders saw how three emerging technologies — wireless LANs (local area networks), voice recognition, and a hands-free communication badge — could be combined to redefine how mobile workers communicated within a facility, replacing clumsy pagers and noisy overhead announcement systems. A worker using Vocera's product could contact any other worker by touching a single button and stating the name of the person to whom they wanted to speak. The business model was based on enterprise sales: Vocera would sell the hardware badges and license the software. The only problem was that Vocera was not sure who, if anyone, had an acute enough pain to actually pay for the solution. After brainstorming potential verticals and then conducting targeted focus groups, they hit gold with hospitals and medical facilities They have continued to evolve their offering to meet that market's need.

Business Model Undefined (examples: Salesforce and Redbox)

SALESFORCE's founder Mark Benioff had a big vision of software being delivered as a service (SaaS) and fundamentally changing the way enterprise software was developed and distributed. The company he founded, Salesforce.com, exploited the Internet to achieve this, and had to develop a multi-tenant platform to create economies of scale. [84] The initial solution could have been applied to any enterprise application, but CRM (Customer Relationship Management) emerged as the top candidate for SaaS delivery. Salesforce now had to test its hypothesis. Its initial solution did not need better features and functions than products that already existed in the marketplace. The entire feature set was already defined by the major players at the time, such as Seibel Systems (later acquired by Oracle), which was already in the CRM space.

Salesforce, however, wasn't selling licensed software with big upfront fees, yearly maintenance, and the need for an in-house IT staff to maintain the solution. Salesforce's business model was fundamentally different. It sold an on-demand solution, delivered through the Internet. It offered customers three great benefits: a pay-as-you-go model, an attractive price point, and freedom from needing a dedicated IT staff to set-up and maintain the system. The product itself was actually inferior to many of the alternatives. The web did not support dynamic content when Salesforce launched. The user had to manually click a refresh button to see data update on the screen. Further, the Internet could be slow in those days and the time to render new screens often seemed interminably long. But Salesforce wasn't competing on features; it was competing on a new business model and using a new technology to disrupt the status quo. In doing so, Salesforce brought CRM to a whole new market of small and medium sized businesses that could not previously afford an enterprise level CRM solution.

The DVD Kiosk rental company REDBOX started from the solution, which was vending. Vending provides an already established business model. Redbox first tested their system by selling groceries, placing four kiosks in the Washington Metropolitan Area that offered items such as milk, eggs, and sandwiches. Strategically, Redbox also tested a second concept — a DVD rental kiosk. Within

---

84   Before SaaS there were ASPs or Applications Solution Providers. These were single tenant-hosted solutions delivered through the Internet. Although an important evolutionary step to SaaS, ASPs did not fare very well as their cost could not be lowered enough to enable a new segment of the market to participate.

the year, Redbox pulled the grocery kiosks and pivoted to focus the company's full attention on the DVD rental market with their iconic red machine. In 2007, five years after release, Redbox surpassed the leading retail rental chain Blockbuster for number of US locations,[85] which now number 35,000.[86] They have rented over three billion discs to date[87] and have expanded into games.

Vending is often a premium model centered around convenience. But for the DVD market, Redbox pursued a combined convenience and discount strategy. Movies rented for $1 per night, much less than Blockbuster. Further, vending is usually a one-way transaction: the customer buys and consumes the product. Redbox's kiosks had to accommodate the rental DVD being returned. The company also supported the ability to reserve a movie or game in advance.

1.4 Visionary (Type IV)

Business Model Defined (example: Post-it Notes)

POST-IT® brand notes, made by 3M, started as a type III technology-driven product. Dr. Spencer Silver, a 3M chemist, developed the technology, a low tack reusable pressure sensitive adhesive, in 1968. He shopped the idea around 3M for over five years trying to find a problem that the adhesive could solve. In 1974, his co-worker Art Fry saw the potential. Fry sang in his church choir and was frustrated when the bookmarks he used to mark the different hymns to be sung fell out of the book. Fry believed Spencer's adhesive could be used to create a reusable bookmark.[88] Employees within the company liked the bookmark, but didn't start using them in large volumes. Then one day, Fry cut out part of a sticky bookmark and posted a note with a question on the front of the report he was writing. This was Fry's eureka moment — before long, 3M staffers could not get enough samples of this new version of the product.[89]

---

85   http://en.wikipedia.org/wiki/Redbox
86   http://www.redbox.com/facts
87   http://www.redbox.com/history
88   "Art Fry and Spencer Silver: Post-it® notes", Inventor of the Week, Lemel-Son MIT, (http://web. mit.edu/invent/iow/frysilver.html)
89   A. Fry, S. Silver, and S. Duguid, "First Person: We invented the Post-it Note", FT.com, December 3, 2010 (http://www.ft.com/cms/s/2/f08e8a9a-fcd7-11df-ae2d-00144feab49a.html#axzz18hyDnyKX)

3M launched Post-it notes in four cities in 1977. Sales were disappointing: consumers did not directly understand the problem the Post-it solved and how useful the product could be. The team realized they needed to give out samples. When they did so in Boise, Idaho, users rated their intent to repurchase at 95%.[90] The team knew they had a success on their hands. The product launched nationally in 1980, and within two years Post-it notes were considered a necessity in every office, alongside pens and paperclips.[91]

The business model for Post-its was clear. 3M sold many office products such as Scotch® tape and glue sticks through office supply companies and retail stores. Post-it Notes used 3M's existing distribution and sales channels to reach the customer.

Business Model Undefined (examples: Xerox and Twitter)

XEROX, founded in 1906, developed technology that, decades later, made plain paper photocopying possible with the launch of the Xerox 914 photocopier in 1959.[92] The equipment was large, weighing almost 650 pounds, and expensive.[93] Before commercializing the technology, Xerox approached IBM about selling its patents. IBM commissioned Arthur D. Little, Inc. (ADL), a well-regarded technology and management consultancy in Cambridge, MA. ADL concluded that if the photocopier displaced 100% of the carbon paper and dittograph market, it would not justify the expense of commercializing the product. Further, the copiers would be out of reach of most business budgets, limiting the total market. We all know the end of this story. ADL got it completely wrong. Xerox created an entirely new market and grew to be an industry titan. IBM never entered the photocopier market.

How could ADL's analysis have missed the mark by such a wide margin? ADL staff had plenty of intellectual horsepower, but they were being asked to forecast a market in the visionary quadrant, where user behavior cannot easily be predicted. In the average office in 1959, secretaries typed documents (word processors did not exist yet). When more than one document was required they inserted carbon paper between multiple sheets of paper. When they made a mistake, they

----

90   Ibid.
91   Ibid. "Art Fry and Spencer Silver: Post-it® notes", Inventor of the Week
92   The copier could reproduce a 9"x14"
93   http://en.wikipedia.org/wiki/Xerox_914

had to manually correct the original and each of the copies one at a time. The terms "cc" and "bcc" (*carbon copy* and *blind carbon copy*), as used in email, are vestiges of this era. Offices had other processes that seem unimaginable from today's perspectives. They had central filing systems that secretaries indexed and meticulously maintained. Because copies were so hard to make, originals were sent around in interoffice envelopes with distribution lists attached. When the first person on the list read the notice, they crossed their name off and put the envelope back in interoffice mail to go to the next person on the list. This cycle repeated until everyone on the list had received the notice.

In hindsight, we can see that a secretary would love to be able to type once and copy as many times as they wanted. Further, if they made a mistake, how wonderful to correct only the master and run off a new set of copies. Likewise, why slowly pass around an original when you can easily make and give everyone their own copy? But to see the possible is to see first that the current process could be improved.

Xerox also made a brilliant move in structuring its business model. They adopted a "razor and blade" strategy. Knowing most companies could not afford or would not budget to purchase an expensive photocopier, Xerox placed the machines for free and charged for copies. This allowed users to learn all the interesting uses for a photocopier. Once people got a taste of how powerful the Xerox machine was, usage grew and grew.

The concept for **TWITTER** emerged from a day-long brainstorming session at podcasting company Odeo. The assumption was that a service that allowed an individual to communicate by broadcasting a 140 character SMS messages would be useful.[94] The service initially gained little traction when it launched in 2006. Nine months later in 2007, Twitter negotiated to have two large flat panel displays placed in the hallways of Austin's South by Southwest (SXSW) music festival to display tweets about the conference by conference attendees.[95] Usage spiked. Twitter reached a critical mass of users. Within a short time after, tweeting would enter into the cultural lexicon of America and much of the world.

Beyond conferences, Tweeting had a tribal appeal, allowing users to coordinate their social activities on a Friday night, break and share news stories, get an

---

94   http://en.wikipedia.org/wiki/Twitter
95   http://www.quora.com/What-is-the-process-involved-in-launching-a-start-up-at-SXSW

insight into the lives of public figures and chat about live TV events. Celebrities discovered it as a way to engage their fan-base. Twitter was even used to mobilize social revolutionaries and force regime change in the Middle East during the Arab Spring.[96]

It wasn't until 2010, four years after launch, that Twitter attempted to seriously monetize its user base with an advertising model of promoted trends and tweets.[97] The company posted $2.2 billion in revenue in 2015.[98] As of March 2016, Twitter had over 310 million active users per month[99] sending over 500 million tweets per day.[100] Could Jack Dorsey and his co-founders have created a financial forecast for Twitter when they founded the company in March 2006? Could the team even have created an accurate product roadmap? For those in the visionary quadrant, it is highly unlikely.

----
96   http://en.wikipedia.org/wiki/Twitter_usage
97   J.P. Mangalindan, "Twitter's business model: a visionary experiment", CNNMoney.com, July 9, 2010.
(http://money.cnn.com/2010/07/09/magazines/fortune/Twitter_business_model.fortune/index.htm)
98   *Twitter Inc. Form 10-K filed 2/29/2016 for period ending 12/31/2015*, p. 39
99   https://about.twitter.com/company
100   http://www.internetlivestats.com/twitter-statistics/

ABOUT THE AUTHOR

Greg is a 20-year Product Management veteran with extensive experience in understanding customer needs and collaborating with development to create market-driven products. He is an expert and strong advocate of customer centric design, Agile development, and a pioneer of Lean product management methods.

He has worked and consulted to venture start-ups and large companies alike, including Software-as-a-Service (SaaS) products, data analytics, and medical diagnostics and devices. Companies include Accretive Health, Chiron Diagnostics, Cisco, Computer Associates, Dell, Experian, ideaLab!, Instill, Kaiser, Mako Surgical, Pandesic, People Fluent, Smith and Nephew Endoscopy, SunTrust, and Walmart.com.

Greg is the author of the books *Agile Excellence for Product Managers, Lean Product Management*, and *42 Rules of Product Management*, the former president of the Silicon Valley Product Management Association, as well as a speaker and frequent commentator on product management issues.

Greg earned an MBA with honor from Babson College and a Bachelor of Science in Mechanical Engineering with second major in Electrical Engineering from Tufts University.

INDEX

Made in the USA
San Bernardino, CA
07 October 2017